EXAM *Revision*

AS/A-LEVEL

Economics

John Hearn

2nd Edition

Philip Allan Updates, an imprint of Hodder Education, part of Hachette Livre UK, Market Place, Deddington, Oxfordshire OX15 0SE

Orders

Bookpoint Ltd, 130 Milton Park, Abingdon, Oxfordshire OX14 4SB
tel: 01235 827720
fax: 01235 400454
e-mail: uk.orders@bookpoint.co.uk

Lines are open 9.00 a.m.–5.00 p.m., Monday to Saturday, with a 24-hour message answering service. You can also order through the Philip Allan Updates website:
www.philipallan.co.uk

© Philip Allan Updates 2008

ISBN 978-0-340-95856-8

First printed 2008
Impression number   5   4   3   2   1
Year   2013   2012   2011   2010   2009   2008

Printed in Spain

Hachette Livre UK's policy is to use papers that are natural, renewable and recyclable products and made from wood grown in sustainable forests. The logging and manufacturing processes are expected to conform to the environmental regulations of the country of origin.

Contents

Unit 2 Macroeconomics for AS: national and international economics

Unit 3 Microeconomics for A2: the economics of business

Unit 4 Macroeconomics for A2: the national and global economy

The revision process

Using revision notes

Before you look at these revision notes, you will have read the recommended textbooks, written your own notes and, where relevant, constructed essays, answered multiple-choice and data response questions and generally felt knowledgeable about each part of the course as you studied it. The examinations are now getting closer and it is time to put together all your notes and start a revision programme.

Most A-level courses in economics require you to cover the whole syllabus. Certain papers give you no choice of questions; you have to answer them all. This volume of revision notes covers the entire course. The notes are not exhaustive — they are **prompts to your memory**, foundations which can support the rest of your knowledge and catalysts to your thought processes.

It is likely that you will have important tests throughout your course and it is possible to use the revision notes in preparing for these tests as well as for the final examinations, but only after you have completed all the groundwork.

All economics examinations require you to show two broad skills. First, you must thoroughly understand economics to the level where you can answer multiple choice questions, and not feel, as many unprepared students do, that they are multiple-guess questions. Second, you must be able to **express your knowledge** of economics clearly and concisely to an examiner in the form of short answers and essays.

Revision notes are an important step towards achieving your best in the examination. The final step, however, is how you apply this knowledge in response to data, case studies and essay questions. You must look upon these revision notes as the first part of the final stage in your preparations. These notes will not tell you how to write essays or respond to data questions but, without the appropriate knowledge, you will not be able to complete the final steps successfully.

Many examination questions require you to **apply economic theory** to a real world situation. Writing about the real world situation without showing a clear understanding of the economic theory will gain very few marks. For example, if you are asked about privatising the National Health Service, it is no good releasing all those pent-up emotions and conducting a political diatribe. You are an economist and you must look at supply, demand, market places, optimal and efficient resource allocation. You must ask questions about whether the product of the NHS is a private good. Does it have significant externalities which class it as a merit good? Are parts of the service public goods, for example the prevention of contagious disease? If this is so, then economics implies that taxation is the only efficient way to provide public goods. If you provide the service free, how do you deal with the problem of consumers using the product up to the point where marginal utility is zero?

This is what these revision notes will do for you. They will give you the economist's perspective. There are brief notes on all the basic theory. Important terms are defined and important diagrams are set in context.

The revision plan

At least 1 month before the examination you need to devise a **revision plan**, and then you need to **stick to it**. Divide up the course into manageable portions and aim to complete the revision process a week before the examination. This gives you some leeway in case you are unwell or an unexpected event leaves you unable to complete a day or two of revision.

Remember that some of your examinations will be in the morning and your brain will need to be functioning early in the day. Get used to rising early and going to sleep before midnight. It takes several weeks for the body to settle into a routine and you do not want to be at your best at 9.00 p.m. and at your worst at 9.00 a.m.

As an economist you know the trade-off between **investment** and **consumption**. Look upon completing your revision plan as investment in your future. Consumer activities like clubs, cinemas, etc. will raise your standard of living during the last month before your exams, but forego this consumption, invest in your future and you are likely to raise your standard of living for the rest of your life.

Ergonomics and economics

Ergonomics studies the efficiency of people in their working environment and it has been found that efficiency can be significantly raised by **working in the right way**. If you have not already done so, get organised! **Minimise disturbance to maximise returns**. The revision process requires a little reading and a lot of writing — you do not communicate with the examiner orally or through telepathy, but by how well you can write.

Locate a table and chair (not too comfortable) facing a wall — not a window — and eliminate all possible distractions. Some students argue in favour of music while they revise. If you are listening to the music, you are not revising. If the music is drowning out other extraneous noises, then it could be an advantage to play music without lyrics by an artist you do not like.

As you revise, separate what you already know from what you have forgotten. By skimming through this book you can identify areas which require you to return to the main text. **Time is at a premium** and you need not waste it by rereading what you already know. Get permission to place a lot of lists around the house — one of the best places is behind the toilet door.

The day of the examination

Remember to wear comfortable clothes and take some extra clothing just in case it is colder than expected. Nice warm feet are a real bonus during the examination. It is better to look like a 'dork' and feel comfortable than to act like one.

As well as the obligatory sweets and bottled water, do not forget pens, pencils, erasers, rulers, a watch and two calculators or one with fresh batteries.

You will already know the structure of the examination paper, how many questions you need to answer and roughly how much time to allocate to each question. Once in the examination room, check all these details are correct and **manage your time efficiently**.

The most common criticism of students by examiners is that they do not answer the set question. **Read the question carefully** and separate relevant from irrelevant detail. It is frustrating that you know so much and only a small fraction of your knowledge can be used in the examination, but do not fall into the trap of writing all you know — **only write what is relevant**.

The single most important rule of examinations should be obvious: **never leave the examination room before the end of your allotted time**. You only get one chance to communicate to the examiner that you deserve a grade A. Do not waste the opportunity. Remember that deep down inside everyone there is a creative person waiting to get out. If you feel you have absolutely nothing more to say, then let your creative juices flow. Look for ways of amplifying the points you have made, add examples from your own experiences and, where discussion is an option, do not be afraid to question the answers as well as answer the questions.

If you inadvertently press the panic button, then close your eyes and count to 30. Your mind will clear, the override will kick in and new ideas will come flooding in. No matter how hard or easy the examination seems, do not give up. Remember that your *relative* performance, rather than your *absolute* performance, is important. If everyone finds the examination difficult, there is a good chance that pass rates and grade boundaries will be lowered. If the paper is easy, standards will be higher.

Exam revision notes structure

It is traditional to divide economics into microeconomics and macroeconomics. Microeconomics looks at the small economic unit, the individual, the household, the firm. The chosen unit is put under the economist's microscope and analysed in detail, while the rest of the economic system is held constant (ceteris paribus) on the assumption that the relative neglect will not lead to serious error. Often these studies are referred to as partial equilibrium analysis. Macroeconomics looks at large economic units such as the national economy and international groups like the European Union. This is often referred to as general equilibrium analysis.

When students come across this division, they should remember that in reality studies in economics range between two finite extremes: the small unit (individual) to the large unit (world) and there is no clear point of division.

All macroeconomic analysis can be broken down into its microeconomic components and vice versa. Most of the world now accepts that the model of a market economy illustrates a better way of allocating resources than is possible in a planned or command economy. However, it is not perfect and markets have imperfections and even fail completely to allocate resources in any satisfactory way for certain products.

The AS is divided into two parts, and the first section of the revision notes will reflect this under the first two unit headings:

Unit 1 Microeconomics for AS: markets, market imperfections and market failures
Unit 2 Macroeconomics for AS: national and international economics

In order to complete the A-level two further units will have to be studied at A2. Unit 3 will comprise more advanced work in microeconomics and will include the economics

of work and leisure, of transport and of business in general. Unit 4 will involve more macroeconomics and will look at countries in the wider context of groups of countries, and the process of globalisation as an increasing number of countries accept interaction rather than isolation. These two units are described as synoptic and therefore draw upon the knowledge gained at AS, with more advanced theoretical analysis and more evaluation through discussion and comment. Therefore the second part of this revision book will look at the A2 units:

Unit 3   Microeconomics for A2: the economics of business
Unit 4   Macroeconomics for A2: the national and global economy

You may have played the game in which a tray of objects is placed in front of you for a few seconds and then is taken away. The test is to recall as many objects as you can. Because the objects are randomly chosen with no obvious relationship, it is difficult to remember them, though you will have committed a few to short-term memory. If you are given a picture of a house to look at for a similar length of time and then asked to describe it, you will remember more because a house has an easily recognisable structure. Even more interesting is the effect on your longer-term memory. If, after several days, you are asked to recall the tray of objects, you will probably have forgotten all of them. However, if you are asked to describe the house in the picture, you will remember much more. If you can see economics as a structure that fits together, it will be much easier to revise and recall the relevant information in an examination.

Throughout these revision notes, headings are weighted. Each of the four units is subdivided as follows:

Main headings	A	B	C
Subdivided	**1**	**2**	**3**
Subdivided again	**1.1**	**1.2**	**1.3**
Subdivided yet again	**1.1a**	**1.1b**	**1.1c**

Given this structure, it should be easy to identify how things fit together. Each page is split so that the main body of text is separated from a 'comments' column which is used to highlight important and interesting points. In the main text, important terms are emboldened to attract your attention. For those students studying the A-level in a modular form, the A-level board specification and their own notes will direct them to the relevant parts of this revision book.

The labelling of diagrams

Throughout the book, where a diagram measures only one thing on the vertical axis, e.g. price on a supply and demand diagram, then that variable is labelled. However, where more than one thing can be measured from that axis, e.g. marginal cost and average revenue, or in the case of macroeconomics, the nominal values of withdrawals and injections, then the currency sign (£) will appear on the vertical axis. This signals that more than one variable can be nominally measured from that axis.

Acknowledgements

I must recognise a debt of gratitude to the following people: the economists whose textbooks I have used in the past — Lipsey, Stanlake, Begg et al; those inspirational economists Smith, Keynes, Friedman and Hayek who made me think; my colleagues, particularly Martin Tucker and Stuart Luker; my students, who have kept me on my intellectual toes; my sons, Ben and Chris, who were also my students; and above all my wife, Geraldine, who types, edits and reorganises all my work.

John Hearn

A The nature and scope of economics

1 Definitions

There are many definitions of economics linked to scarcity and the allocation of resources. Arguably the most quoted definition is that from Lionel Robbins who wrote that economics is:

> If you want to impress your examiner, learn this quote. It comes from 'An Essay on the Nature and Significance of Economic Science' (Lord Robbins).

'...the science which studies human behaviour as a relationship between ends and scarce means which have alternative use.'

2 The economic problem

> In this context, economic goods include services. Economics studies these allocative mechanisms in detail.

Economic problems like inflation and unemployment are symptoms of (and therefore should not be confused with) **the economic problem**. The economic problem is **scarcity**, i.e. not enough resources to satisfy everyone's demand. All **economic goods** are scarce, some more and some less so, but all require an **allocative mechanism**. The only goods that do not require an allocative mechanism are **free goods**. An example of a free good is air, although it is interesting to note that in a polluted city like Los Angeles fresh air is likely to become an economic good.

Given a limited ability to obtain resources, both **consumers** and **producers** must choose between alternative products. Scarcity leads to **choice** and in theory it is assumed that, in a free market, economic units make **rational decisions**.

> Look at Eastern Europe during the Communist era.

In a centrally controlled economy the aim is to maximise the **total welfare** of society. In reality, the sheer size of an undertaking which tries to match the sum of individual demands and direct resources to them has led to the **decline** of this allocative mechanism.

3 Political systems and the economics of resource allocation

3.1 Introduction

All economies require allocative mechanisms. At the theoretical extremes, economies are divided into:
- **free market or capitalist**
- **centrally-controlled or command**

In reality all countries are a mixture of central direction and marketplaces. More freedom in markets and the economy will be described as capitalist; more control in markets and the economy will be described as command. In command economies a lot of trade takes place on illegal or black markets.

3.2 Free market capitalism

Minimal government is concerned with creating a framework of rules that protects:
- **freedom of contract**
- **private property rights**

> In the past, slavery meant people were owned.

Producers are free to buy, hire and own non-human factors of production but only to hire and fire labour. They compete in product and productive factor markets.

> Producer sovereignty is a market imperfection caused by monopolies.

Consumer sovereignty determines what is produced, who produces it and how it is produced. The marketplace is where the **invisible hand** of competition will harness the self-interest of the individual so that society benefits from the pursuit of **profit**. The invisible hand is a powerful concept in economics, first introduced by Adam Smith in his book, *Wealth of Nations*, published in 1776.

3.3 The command economy

Government tries to solve the economic problem by total planning. There are no rights to own property. Incomes are received for work, not as the result of ownership. Production and productive factors need to be under the direction of a central authority. Quotas are established for productive units. Consumption by workers can be directed through vouchers used as a part share of planned output.

> In the heyday of the command economy, some economists estimated that between 30% and 50% of all trade was through black markets.

Alternatively incomes can be awarded through central planning and consumers can choose how to spend their incomes. The marketplace must be part of a system aimed at bringing about an equitable distribution of resources. Therefore, prices may be fixed and shortages and surpluses used as signals to expand or contract output.

Many command economies are currently going through a transitional phase as they free up their markets to competition. This has caused a number of problems as their industries are not competitive. Many of their resources need to be shifted from state bureaucracy and producer goods like armaments to the provision of consumer goods.

3.4 The mixed economy

3.4a The disadvantages of free market capitalism
- Instability in the form of **booms** and **recessions**.
- Product sovereignty caused by powerful single firm industries.
- **Inequalities:** millionaires and beggars.

> Externalities are a very important concept throughout economics.

- **Externalities:** uncontracted costs or benefits which are not paid for when goods are produced or consumed.

3.4b The disadvantages of a command economy
- Lack of incentive in pursuing collectivist ideals.

> Would you work harder if you were to get an individual grade at A-level or an average grade for the group?

- **A paradox of equality.** On the surface it is easy to create an equality of ownership by removing private property — it is not so easy to ensure an even distribution of the resources that make up a person's standard of living.

In Moscow in the 1970s, it was reported that Muscovites spent several hours every day in queues.

- Resource misallocation as consumer demand is not satisfied by producer supply.
- Shortages, and rationing through a queuing system.

3.5 The market economy

All the world's major economies are now classed as market economics, although the degrees of intervention by government vary greatly, depending upon their perception of the extent to which free markets are imperfect or fail to allocate resources.

4 Optimality and efficiency

Vilfredo Pareto, 1848–1923.

4.1 Pareto optimality

Most students know that a best case exists when the economy's resources are allocated in such a way that no reallocation can make anyone better off without making someone else worse off. However, they do not know how it is achieved. There are three maximising conditions:

Optimal comes from the Latin *optimus*, which means 'best'.

- An optimal distribution of products between consumers requires that:

$$\frac{MUXA}{MUYA} = \frac{MUXB}{MUYB}$$

where MU = marginal utility
X and Y = products
A and B = consumers

- Optimal allocation of productive factors occurs where:

$$\frac{MPLX}{MPCX} = \frac{MPLY}{MPCY}$$

where MP = marginal product
X and Y = products
C and L = productive factors

- Optimal output is where:

$$\frac{MUX}{MCX} = \frac{MUY}{MCY}$$

where MU = marginal utility
X and Y = products
MC = marginal cost

This is explained in more detail under Microeconomics for A2.

4.2 Economic efficiency

There are three types of efficiency commonly referred to:

- **allocative efficiency:** firms produce where price equals marginal cost
- **productive efficiency:** firms produce at the lowest average cost
- **dynamic efficiency:** firms reduce costs over time

5   The opportunity cost of resource allocation

One of the most important concepts in economics is **opportunity cost**. It is fitting to complete this first section by identifying its relevance to the analysis so far and highlighting its importance to the study of economics in general.

- Opportunity cost is a real measure in terms of the foregone alternative at the level of either production or consumption.

All the time that products and productive factors are scarce in economic terms, then transactions can be measured by opportunity cost. There is one good which is not scarce and therefore does not have an opportunity cost: **the free good**.

All economic goods have an opportunity cost of production. When they are provided free to the consumer, they do not have an opportunity cost of consumption.

These products are explained in more detail under Unit 1, Section F.

Type of product	Opportunity cost of production	Opportunity cost of consumption
Free good	No	No
Public good	Yes	No
Merit good	Yes	No
Club good	Yes	Yes
Private good	Yes	Yes

Opportunity cost is often illustrated using a **production possibility boundary** (Figure 1.1).

This is the first diagram in these notes. It is therefore timely to remind you that all diagrams must be drawn correctly with full labelling. Written work can be considerably enhanced by clear illustrations that are both correct and relevant.

*Figure 1.1
Production possibility
boundary*

The line *AB* represents the maximum quantity or combination of consumer and capital goods that can be produced given current resources. If Y_1X_1 represents current output, then the opportunity cost of moving from Y_1 to Y_2 is a contraction from X_1 to X_2.

B The theory of demand

1 *The concepts used in demand analysis*

1.1 Utility

1.1a Introduction
Utility is defined as a measure of the satisfaction which is derived from the consumption of a good or service. The units of measurement are known as 'utils'.

Consumer theory is based upon the assumption that individuals will arrange their pattern of expenditure to maximise utility.

> In reality most individuals will admit to purchasing something which gave them little or no satisfaction. This is usually explained by imperfect knowledge or pressure from advertising.

1.1b The law of diminishing utility
Over a specific period of time and assuming the consumption of other products is fixed, the utility derived from consuming successive units of the same product will add less to a rising total and may even reduce total utility past a certain level of consumption.

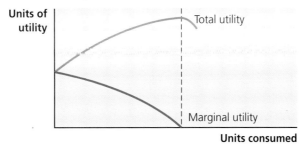

Figure 1.2

> A common mistake is to write that marginal utility rises before it starts to fall.

Figure 1.2 shows that marginal utility is falling as total utility rises by ever decreasing amounts.

1.1c Can utility be measured?
It may seem strange to be asking this question after diagrams have been drawn. However, in reality it is not possible to measure utility in any meaningful way that allows comparisons between one consumer and another. It is, though, much easier to rank products for each individual consumer. Their expenditure reflects the expected utility that will be derived from each unit of money spent.

> Alfred Marshall (1842–1924) solved the problem.

1.1d The paradox of value
Some early economists were confused by the fact that people were prepared to pay high prices for non-essential goods like diamonds when they spent little or nothing on essential goods like water.

The confusion was generated by looking at the high marginal utility from the last diamond and the low marginal utility from the last drop of water. The answer was found by looking at relative scarcity and the total utility derived from each product. The total utility from water was much greater than the total utility from diamonds, as shown in Figures 1.3(a) and 1.3(b). Where the sum of the marginal

utility for water is far greater than for diamonds, and because diamonds command a price, they would be consumed at much lower quantity Q_1 in Figure 1.3(a), whereas water, if it is free to the consumer will be consumed at a much higher level Q_1 in Figure 1.3(b).

Ask yourself this question: You are dying of thirst in the desert and one glass of water can save your life. Someone offers you either water or the world's biggest diamond. Which will you take?

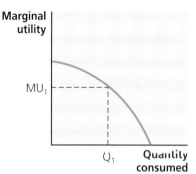

Figure 1.3(a) Marginal utility schedule for diamonds

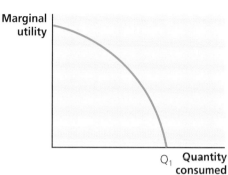

Figure1.3(b) Marginal utility schedule for water

1.2 The budget line

The budget line joins together different combinations of X and Y that can be purchased given a fixed sum of money (Figure 1.4).

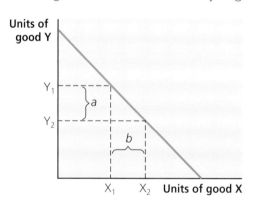

Figure 1.4

The slope of the budget line identifies the opportunity cost of more X or more Y.

Opportunity cost of X $= \dfrac{a}{b}$

Opportunity cost of Y $= \dfrac{b}{a}$

Parallel shifts in the budget line occur if income changes or if each price changes by the same percentage.

The **slope** of the budget line changes when relative prices change, i.e. one price changes by a different percentage to the other.

2 *Consumer theory: the individual demand curve*

The demand curve for an individual establishes the functional relationship between the price of a product and the quantity demanded.

This is a very simple example, but we will use the same numbers to build up a more complex model. If you get lost, then keep going back to pick up the argument.

This can be illustrated in its simplest form if we assume a person has only £50 to spend on one product and total utility increases with each successive purchase. Table 1.1 shows how many will be purchased at various prices.

Table 1.1

Price	Quantity demanded
£50	1
£25	2
£10	5
£5	10

I will leave you to graph this function, remembering that the convention is price on the vertical axis and quantity on the horizontal axis.

Now let us make it a little more difficult by assuming the consumer has a choice of two products X and Y, the same expenditure constraint, i.e. £50, and a price for both products of £5. In order to answer this, let us use some made-up numbers for marginal utility (Table 1.2).

Table 1.2

Units consumed	Marginal utility of X	Marginal utility of Y
1st	20	15
2nd	18	12
3rd	16	10
4th	14	8
5th	12	6
6th	11	5
7th	10	2
8th	4	1
9th	3	0
10th	1	0

The answer is that the consumer will purchase 7X and 3Y and will maximise utility at 138 utils. No other pattern of expenditure can achieve this total.

To work this out, you can proceed in an iterative way, i.e. the first purchase of X gives 20, the second purchase gives 18 and so on until all the money is gone. Alternatively, you can search for the expenditure pattern which spends all the money and equals the marginal utility of the last pound spent on X and Y, i.e.:

$$\frac{\text{marginal utility of X (MUX)}}{\text{price of X (PX)}} = \frac{\text{marginal utility of Y (MUY)}}{\text{price of Y (PY)}} = \frac{10}{5}$$

The analysis is made more complex if we assume a change in relative prices. Suppose the price of X rises to £10 and the same expenditure constraint remains. To approach this in an iterative way, notice that doubling the price of X halves the utility from each pound spent.

Using $\dfrac{\text{MUX}}{\text{PX}} = \dfrac{\text{MUY}}{\text{PY}} = \dfrac{16}{10} = \dfrac{8}{5}$

the answer is 3X and 4Y with utility maximised at 99 utils.

3 Market demand

3.1 The normal product demand curve

'Horizontal sum' means you are adding up on the horizontal axis while the vertical axis remains constant.

The total demand for an individual product is referred to as the market demand. It is the horizontal sum of each individual demand curve and its normal shape is downward sloping from left to right.

The uneven distribution of income in a country like the UK will mean that as the price falls, so more consumers will be able to enter the market. Each consumer will also gain more utility per pound spent as the price falls and will therefore increase consumption as purchases are rearranged to maximise utility.

3.2 Shifts and movements in a demand curve

If the first thing that changes in the relationship between price and quantity demanded is **price**, then this will be represented by a **movement** along the demand curve. If it is **quantity demanded**, then this will be represented by a **shift** in the demand curve.

You need to get this clear. It is one of the first signs that you are going to be a good economist.

A movement along a demand curve occurs as the result of a change in price, whereas more or less of the product demanded at the same price constitutes a shift.

Consider one final variation to make sure you have got this right: **more or less demanded at different prices is a movement; more or less demanded at the same price is a shift.**

Shifts in the demand curve can be the result of:
- rising real income
- economic growth
- change in consumer tastes
- new products entering the market
- new ways of buying and selling, e.g. the internet
- the cost of loans
- advertising
- changes in the price of other competing or complementary products
- changes in the structure or size of the population

3.3 Normal goods and inferior goods

Normal goods have two characteristics:
- The quantity demanded is negatively related to price, i.e. a fall in price raises demand.
- The quantity demanded is positively related to income, i.e. a rise in income raises demand.

By definition an inferior good must have a superior alternative.

Inferior goods have only one characteristic:
- The quantity demanded is negatively related to income, i.e. a rise in income causes a fall in demand.

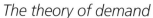
It is common to identify two types of inferior good, one of which has a normal demand curve while the other has a perverse demand curve. The distinguishing feature is the relative strength of the income effect of the price change.

It is important to understand that a change in price has two effects:
- It changes **real income** by raising or lowering spending power.
- It causes a **substitution** of one product for others as the utility per pound spent changes.

Although these two effects take place simultaneously, their separation clearly identifies the two types of inferior good.

4 Price elasticity of demand

4.1 Introduction

The elasticity coefficient measures the responsiveness of a change in demand to a change in price.

Theoretically this relationship is precise and relatively easy to calculate, while in reality the inclusion of many more variables than just price and quantity demanded make it impossible to identify with the precision implied by theory.

Point elasticity: every point along a demand curve has an elasticity value that can be calculated using a ruler. All you have to do is measure the projected distance from the point to the quantity axis and divide it by the projected distance to the price axis (Figure 1.5).

For those of you who find elasticity difficult, there is good news and bad news: point elasticity is simple to understand and very helpful, but does not attract examination questions.

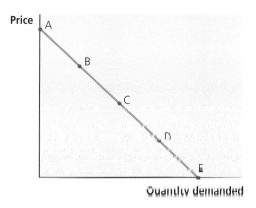

Figure 1.5

$$\text{Point A} = \frac{AE}{A} = \text{infinity}$$

$$\text{Point B} = \frac{BE}{BA} = \text{elastic}$$

$$\text{Point C} = \frac{CE}{CA} = \text{unitary}$$

$$\text{Point D} = \frac{DE}{DA} = \text{inelastic}$$

$$\text{Point E} = \frac{E}{EA} = \text{zero}$$

It is a common mistake to assume that a straight line has uniform elasticity.

Doing this reminds you that every straight line has a different elasticity at every point. If the line is not straight, use tangents to make the calculations.

4.2 The algebra

The universal equation that you must familiarise yourself with is:

$$\text{price elasticity coefficient of demand (c)} = -\frac{\text{percentage change in quantity demanded}}{\text{percentage change in price}}$$

An alternative calculation using averages is:

$$c = -\frac{\text{average price} \times \text{change in quantity demanded}}{\text{change in price} \times \text{average quantity}}$$

All calculations produce a positive answer and strictly there must be a minus sign in front of the percentage changes.

Both calculations produce slightly different answers as one is a percentage change from one point to another whereas the other is the average of a number of points. Do not worry about this — either answer will be accepted.

4.3 The graphs

As well as the straight line in Figure 1.5, there are three **uniform** shapes.

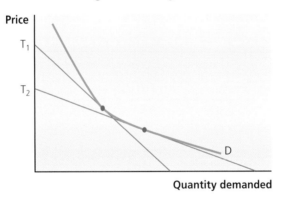

Figure 1.6
The unitary curve

The shape in Figure 1.6 is a rectangular hyperbola. Although it is a curve, each point is equidistant from each axis along the tangents T_1 and T_2 and therefore it has a constant value of 1.

Figure 1.7
The perfectly elastic and perfectly inelastic curves

D_1 **is perfectly inelastic (0):** as price changes there is no change in demand.
D_2 **is perfectly elastic (infinite):** as the price rises above P_1, demand is zero. At and below P_1, the demand is infinite.

4.4 Expenditure and the price elasticity of demand

Most students will say that demand rises when price goes down. Ask them what happens to expenditure on a product as demand rises and they will usually start by saying that expenditure rises. Place two numbers on the axes and they will realise that selling nothing at £100 or giving away 1,000 at a zero price produces no revenue.

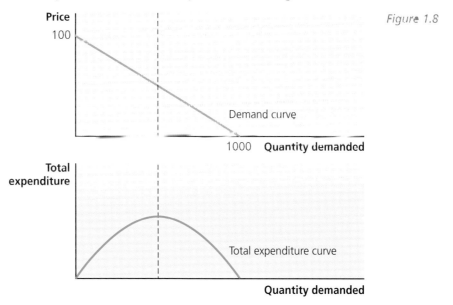

Figure 1.8

Figure 1.8 shows that as price falls there is a range over which:
- demand rises and expenditure rises
- demand rises and expenditure stays the same
- demand rises and expenditure falls

Many firms around the world have gone bankrupt because they do not understand this relationship. Ask a person in business how they will improve profitability. 'Sell more' is usually the answer. How will you sell more? 'Lower the price' may be the answer. As we can see, there is a price range over which this is exactly the **right answer** and a price range over which this is exactly the **wrong answer**.

Another interesting point is illustrated by the unitary demand curve: whatever the price, the expenditure on the product remains unchanged. In Figure 1.9, multiply the price by the quantity sold.

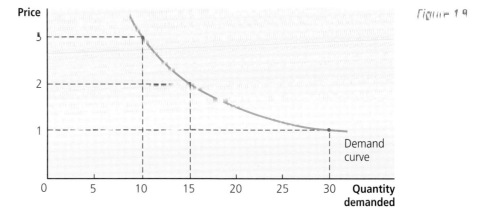

Figure 1.9

4.5 Be thankful for smokers, drinkers and gamblers

We have already pointed out that, in reality, you cannot calculate precisely an elasticity. However, anyone who changes a price does so with some expectation

about the effect it will have on demand. Firms do this all the time, as does the government when changing the indirect tax on a product.

No one should be advised to become a smoker, drinker or gambler, so look back in your main notes to remind yourself why we must all be grateful to them.

5 Cross-price elasticity of demand

Here the + or – signs used to record a rise or fall are important as they are the first sign of the possible type of relationship between two products. A positive or negative cross-price elasticity is a necessary, though on its own not a sufficient, condition to prove the relationship. Products could have changed together but be totally independent.

This is the responsiveness of demand for one product to a change in the price of another product.

The formula is:

$$\text{cross-price elasticity of demand} = \frac{\text{percentage change in demand for X}}{\text{percentage change in the price of Y}}$$

Competitive products which are **substitutes** for each other will have a **positive** cross-price elasticity: a rise in the price of one product will raise demand for the other product.

Products in **complementary** or **derived demand** will have a **negative** cross-price elasticity: a rise in the price of one product will reduce the demand for the other product.

Independent products will have a zero or infinite cross-price elasticity of demand, i.e. a change in one product will not affect the other product.

6 Income elasticity of demand

Income elasticity of demand is the degree of response of demand to a change in income.

The formula is:

In all three elasticity calculations the quantity demanded is on the top. If you remember this, you are less likely to make a mistake.

$$\text{income elasticity of demand} = \frac{\text{percentage change in quantity demanded}}{\text{percentage change in income}}$$

Consumption of a **normal** good will rise as income rises.

Normal goods which are **necessities** will at some point have elasticities which tend towards zero, i.e. at some point as your income rises you will want to stop eating more food. Normal goods which are **luxuries** will produce income elasticities with higher numerical values.

Inferior goods will have income elasticities of demand which are negative because a rise in income will lead to a fall in demand.

C The theory of supply

1 The individual firm's cost and supply curves

1.1 Definitions

Important definitions which need to be clear before we proceed are:

- average total cost — $\dfrac{\text{total cost}}{\text{total output}}$

- average fixed cost $= \dfrac{\text{total fixed cost}}{\text{total output}}$

- average variable cost $= \dfrac{\text{total variable cost}}{\text{total output}}$

- marginal cost $=$ additional cost of producing one more unit

1.2 The firm's supply curve

The following simplifying assumptions apply:
- firms aim to maximise profits
- in Figure 1.10, firms can sell unlimited amounts of their product at a fixed price
- the cost curves are a normal shape

We will question this in section E2.1.

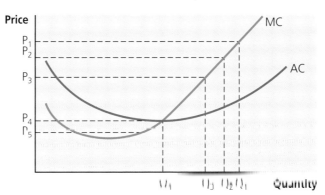

Figure 1.10

The profit maximising rule for a firm is that output will continue to expand until **marginal cost = marginal revenue**.

Marginal revenue is the additional revenue from selling one more unit. In Figure 1.10, **the fixed price means** that price and marginal revenue are equal. Therefore at P_1 the firm will produce at Q_1. As the price falls, output contracts to P_4Q_4. Any price below P_4 will not produce any output in the long run. The reason for this is obvious, as the firm cannot cover its costs and therefore make a profit.

Output can occur in the short run given certain rules that are explained in Unit 3, section C under 'The theories of the firm'.

In this simple example we have proved that the supply curve for a firm is the functional relationship between price and quantity supplied. This function is represented by the **marginal cost curve** where it rises above the **average cost curve**.

2 The industry supply curve

Figure 1.11
Industry supply curve

Under normal circumstances the industry supply curve is upward sloping from left to right. As the industry is a collection of firms, its supply curve is the **horizontal** sum of all the individual firms' supply curves.

3 Shifts and movements in supply curves

If the first thing that changes in the relationship between price and quantity supplied is price, this will be represented by a **movement** along a supply curve. Alternatively, if the first thing that changes is quantity supplied, then this will be represented by a **shift** in the supply curve.

This may be easier to remember in the following form: more or less supplied at **different** prices is a movement; more or less supplied at the **same** price is a shift.

Shifts may occur as the result of:
- weather variability — often related to the agricultural industry
- technical progress
- changes in the price of productive factors
- changes in the price of other factors
- changes in indirect taxation
- changes in subsidies

4 Goods in joint supply

It is a common mistake to assume that demand for these products is also linked.

Goods in joint supply create some interesting special cases as the production of one product inadvertently produces another product. Such goods include:
- wood and sawdust
- lead and zinc
- mutton and wool
- beef and hides
- pork and pigskin

A change in the demand for one of the products shifts the supply curve for the other product.

5 *The elasticity of supply*

5.1 Introduction

Because a certain period of time must elapse before a producer can change the supply of a product, the elasticity also varies over time (Figure 1.12).

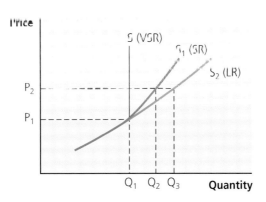

Figure 1.12

In the **very short run**, supply is perfectly inelastic as output cannot change. In the **short run**, output can adjust, but not fully, so the supply function is likely to be more inelastic than in the **long run** when a full adjustment can be made.

5.2 The algebra

As with demand, from a given supply schedule it is possible to calculate a coefficient as a measure of supply elasticity. Again, this determines the relationship between a change in market price and a change in the quantity supplied.

> The slope is positive. It is therefore not necessary to have a minus in front of the equation to produce a positive answer.

The same formulae can be used but adjusted for supply rather than demand. The most common is:

$$c = \frac{\text{percentage change in quantity supplied}}{\text{percentage change in price}}$$

5.3 The graphs

There are three uniform shapes. Two are obvious, namely perfectly elastic and perfectly inelastic, as illustrated in Figure 1.13.

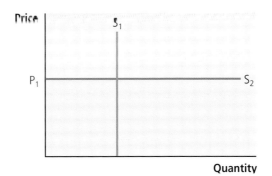

Figure 1.13

> Although this is a theoretical extreme, it is also realistic. There are some products where output cannot change whatever price is offered. An artistic example can be found in the anagram ANILMASO (4,4).

S_1 is **perfectly inelastic** and a rise in price will have no effect on the quantity supplied ($c = 0$).

At price P_1 and above, an infinite quantity will be supplied if the supply curve is **perfectly elastic**, as in S_2. Below P_1 nothing will be supplied (c = infinity).

The third uniform shape is **unitary** supply, which is any straight line that passes through the origin of the graph (Figure 1.14).

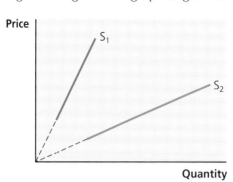

Figure 1.14

Mathematicians can prove this using similar triangles.

Surprisingly, both S_1 and S_2 have the same percentage change on each axis.

Straight lines which would pass through the vertical axis have **elastic** values (greater than one), while straight lines which would pass through the horizontal axis have **inelastic** values (between 0 and 1) (Figure 1.15).

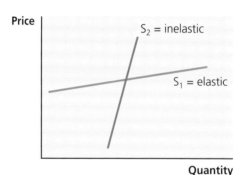

Figure 1.15

5.4 Factors which influence supply elasticity

5.4a Supply elasticity is influenced in the short run by:
- the amount of excess capacity in a firm
- the level of stocks held
- the law of variable proportions
- access to unemployed resources

5.4b Supply elasticity is influenced in the long run by:
- the technology involved in production
- internal and external economies and diseconomies of scale
- access to productive factors

6 *An introduction to theories of the firm*

At AS, an elementary description of the main market structures that supply an economy is required. All the firms in each market structure are assumed to be faced with competing buyers while they are motivated to maximise profits.

The defining characteristics of each theory are set out below.

Perfect competition
- Many firms with no barriers to entry into or exit from the industry.
- Identical products.
- Normal profits in the long run.

Monopolistic competition
- Many firms with no barriers to entry into or exit from the industry.
- Differentiated products.
- Normal profits in the long run

Oligopoly
- A few large firms with barriers to entry and exit.
- Differentiated products.
- The potential to make excessive profits in the long run.

Monopoly
- A single firm industry with barriers to entry.
- The potential to make excessive profits in the long run as the result of being able to set a price.

D The elementary theory of price

1 Equilibrium price and output

Although we have looked independently at supply and demand, in reality they cannot be separated. It is their interaction, without any conscious control, which determines price and output.

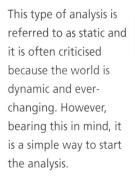

The supply and demand curves have been specially drawn so that they can produce surpluses and shortages using only three quantities. To construct this correctly, draw a square and pass D and S through the corners.

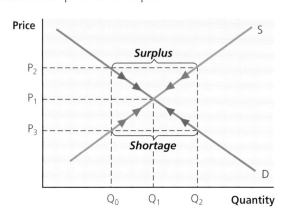

Figure 1.16

An easy way to understand price is to place a normal supply and demand curve on the same diagram (Figure 1.16).

P_1Q_1 is the equilibrium point where **quantity supplied = quantity demanded**.

This equilibrium or point of balance will remain unchanged if nothing else changes. At any other price, forces will be set in motion to move the market back into equilibrium.

This type of analysis is referred to as static and it is often criticised because the world is dynamic and ever-changing. However, bearing this in mind, it is a simple way to start the analysis.

If price is **too high** at P_2, producers will have an incentive to produce more and Q_2 will be produced while only Q_0 is demanded by customers. This surplus will force producers to lower price until the market is cleared.

If price is **too low** at P_3, consumers demand a quantity Q_2, but producers only find it profitable to produce Q_0. This shortage allows producers to raise their price and profits until the market is cleared.

2 Changes in supply and demand functions

In the theories of demand and supply we have explained the difference between a shift and a movement and we have identified the factors which have brought about a shift.

Now that we are looking at the interaction of supply and demand, we need to recognise an important additional point: **a shift in either curve will bring**

about a movement along the other curve. For example, if demand shifts to the right or left, then in order to establish a new equilibrium there will be a movement along the supply curve (Figure 1.17).

In examinations, be careful to use the step-by-step approach. Identify the shift first and then the move-ment. If two things change, then there are likely to be two shifts and two movements.

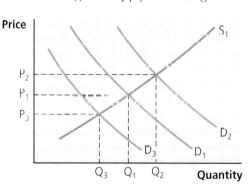

Figure 1.17

The same thing will happen when supply shifts, namely a movement along the demand curve.

3 The cobweb theory: a dynamic theory of price

A theory which is useful in developing price theory, from the simple static inter-pretation so far undertaken to a more realistic analysis in an ever-changing world, is the cobweb theory. Usually applied to agriculture, it uses the static model but introduces a time lag between **decision** and **execution** and an output total that may vary from what was anticipated (e.g. Figure 1.18).

It is important to draw a supply curve which is more inelastic than the demand curve; other-wise the cobweb becomes unstable and moves away from the equilibrium.

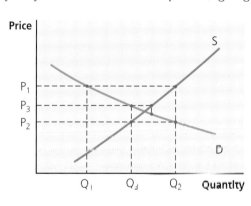

Figure 1.18
Stable cobweb

Suppose a bad harvest produces Q_1. The price will rise to P_1 and P_1 will induce a higher level of output at Q_3. Assuming no more shocks, you can follow the bold points on the curves until you reach the equilibrium.

4 Supply and demand curves and related products

You may be asked a question which looks at the effect on one product of a change in the demand or supply conditions of the related product.

Example 1: What will happen to the price of lead if the demand for zinc increases?

One of the problems with this type of question is that you need to know that lead and zinc both come from the same ore.

To answer this question:
- Make an assumption about the starting equilibrium position for both products.
- Identify the relationship between the products (in this case they are in joint supply).
- Proceed logically through the effects on each product as illustrated below.

The demand curve for zinc will shift to the right as more is demanded at each and every price (Figure 1.19).

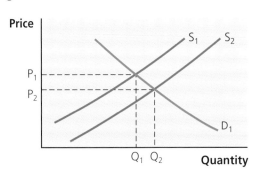

Figure 1.19
The market for zinc

P_1Q_1 = original equilibrium
P_2Q_2 = new equilibriuma at a higher price and significantly a higher output

The supply curve will shift to the right as more is supplied at each and every price (Figure 1.20).

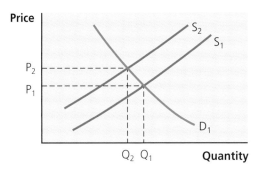

Figure 1.20
The market for lead

P_1Q_1 = original equilibrium
P_2Q_2 = new equilibrium at a higher output and a lower price

Answer: Price of lead falls.

Example 2: What will happen to the price of gas if a war destroys a number of oilfields?

This means less oil will be supplied at each and every price and the supply curve shifts to the left (Figure 1.21).

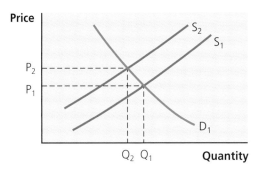

Figure 1.21
The market for oil

P_1Q_1 = original equilibrium

P_2Q_2 = new equilibrium at a lower output and a higher price

Oil and gas are substitutes for each other in the provision of heat and power. The relatively higher price for oil will increase the demand for gas at each and every price (Figure 1.22).

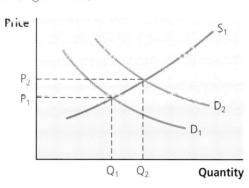

Figure 1.22
The market for gas

P_1Q_1 = original equilibrium

P_2Q_2 = new equilibrium at a higher output and a higher price

Answer: Price of gas rises.

5 The consumer surplus

5.1 Definition

The consumer surplus is the difference between the maximum amount of money a consumer is willing to pay for a product, rather than go without, and the amount actually paid.

Alfred Marshall first identified this in his book, *Principles of Economics* (1890).

5.2 The individual

Suppose an individual would be prepared to pay £10 to buy the first unit of a product, £9 to buy a second unit, £8 to buy a third and £7 to buy a fourth. If the price is £7, the consumer would buy four units costing 4×7 = £28. However, the consumer would have been prepared to pay $10 + 9 + 8 + 7$ = £34. Therefore the consumer surplus is $34 - 28 = 6$.

5.3 The market

If the marketplace produces Figure 1.23, then the shaded area will represent the consumer surplus, i.e. money that consumers would be willing to pay but do not have to as the market price is established at P.

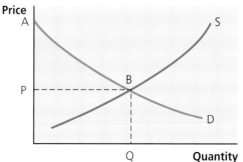

Figure 1.23

PAB = consumer surplus

6 *The producer surplus*

6.1 Definition

The producer surplus is the revenue received by the producer above that which would have brought a particular quantity of the product onto the market for sale.

6.2 The market

In a market analysis it is the difference between the minimum payment that a producer would accept for offering a certain quantity for sale and the market price of the product. In Figure 1.24 it is the shaded area above the supply curve and below the price line.

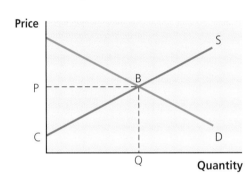

Figure 1.24

PBC = producer surplus

E Some further analysis of price determination and resource allocation

1 Introduction

You should now understand how resources are allocated by prices, which are in turn determined in a marketplace through the interaction of **supply** and **demand**.

This is a very simple analysis and throughout your studies you will have been made aware of factors which have changed or replaced the **price mechanism**.

These factors can be grouped together as those which have:
- influenced supply
- influenced demand
- replaced the market mechanism
- substituted for it in the absence of a marketplace

2 Supply factors which affect the price mechanism

> It is becoming popular to set examination questions which question this assumption.

2.1 Do firms aim to maximise profits?

2.1a A realistic rule?
The assumption that firms maximise profits has been important in the analysis of how firms operate. The profit-maximising rule that firms will produce an output and sell at a price which equates **marginal revenue** with **marginal cost** has been questioned by a number of economists.

2.1b The sales maximisation hypothesis
It is argued, particularly in large firms, that the separation of ownership of the company from its management has led to sales maximisation within a profit constraint.

> This may explain why many firms force their managers to be shareholders and rely on dividends as a significant proportion of their salary.

Managers can justify raising their salaries as firms grow larger, and if the potential for increasing profits is unknown to the majority of shareholders, as may be the case in a **public joint stock company**, then they may be satisfied with a level of profits below maximum.

Figure 1.25 shows that profit maximisation occurs at Pr_1Q_1, but the firm may be able to double its size and still make sufficient profits to satisfy shareholders.

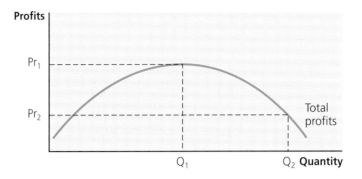

Figure 1.25

Some textbooks go a little further and separate sales revenue maximisation from sales maximisation using a normal profit constraint. The difference between the two is that sales revenue is maximised where marginal revenue is zero, whereas sales maximisation is consistent with normal profit where average cost equals average revenue.

2.1c The sales revenue maximisation hypothesis

As in the previous hypothesis, the firm is willing to accept lower profits, but in this case it is aiming precisely to maximise its sales revenue rather than just accepting a trade off between a higher level of sales and an acceptable level of profits. In this situation, the firm will aim to produce up to the point where its marginal revenue is zero. After this point, any extra sales will reduce total revenue as marginal revenue is negative. So we can conclude that revenue is maximised where MR = 0. It is important to note that revenue maximisation will not produce a profit-maximising position for the firm.

2.1d Satisficing theory

Professor Herbert Simon suggested in satisficing theory that there is **no unique equilibrium**, but rather that firms may have many different goals, including those already stated. Their other targets may include:

● a level of profits which hides potential profits from competitors
● lower profits which avoid short-term embarrassment to a well-known company
● lower profits for environmental reasons
● lower profits for ethical reasons and to identify the company as an ethical investment
● lower prices and profits to reward customer loyalty

A firm may worry about being exposed by Greenpeace or an animal rights organisation and therefore direct some potential profits into environmentally friendly projects.

2.1e Non-maximisation through ignorance

The fact that firms and their customers do not have perfect knowledge and the economic environment is always changing has led some economists to point out that profit maximisation is probably only ever achieved **by luck**. They argue that firms tend to approximate rather than actually achieve.

2.1f Cost-plus pricing

In the 1930s Charles Hitch and Robert Hall made a number of detailed case studies of pricing policy by firms in the Oxford area. They introduced the

Arguably, cost-plus is a short-run response to changes in costs. Demand probably has the final say on pricing in the long run.

hypothesis of **full-cost pricing**. Further empirical studies supported their ideas and gave rise to what is now known as **cost-plus pricing**.

This pricing policy does not equate MC with MR. Instead, it sets price equal to average cost at capacity output plus a conventional mark-up. In this theory prices will tend to be fairly stable and adjust only to changes in costs.

3 Demand factors which affect the price mechanism

3.1 Supply creates demand

Professor J. K. Galbraith suggested that, in certain parts of the market, it is not consumer demand which creates market signals, but large corporations which create and manipulate demand to iron out unexpected changes.

In order to guard against the impact of reductions in demand, companies spend large sums on advertising which allows them to sell what they produce rather than what consumers want to buy.

3.2 Trade unions influence demand

The weakening of trade union power has reduced their influence. However, in the past, successful lobbying of Parliament has led to the imposition of tariffs and quotas on imports to protect and redirect demand in industries such as agriculture, coal mining, shipbuilding and textiles.

F Market imperfections and market failure

1 More imperfections than failure

1.1 Introduction

In reality, markets do not always work perfectly. A lot of time is given in economics to studying imperfections and decisions have to be made as to whether corrective action can improve upon a market. We will look at three situations where the price mechanism does not clear the market.

1.2 Price set too low: potential development of a black market

A good example of this type of market imperfection is when a promoter books a stadium for a rock concert. Rock bands are reputedly temperamental and if the stadium is not full, then the band may refuse to play. The probability of setting a ticket price in advance that will just fill the stadium is very low. There are therefore many examples of prices being set too low, as illustrated in Figure 1.26.

> A black market is often, but not always, an illegal market. It could be a secondary market which clears the market imperfection.

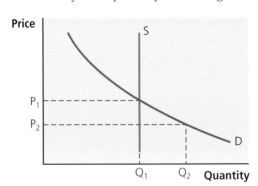

Figure 1.26

P_1 = price that would have cleared the market
Q_1 = fixed number of tickets
P_2 = ticket price
Q_2 = demand for tickets

It may be that the shortage of tickets between Q_1 and Q_2 may leave some customers unsatisfied. Alternatively, if people can get hold of tickets they do not want to use, then a black market will exist where **touting** for higher prices will occur. This may or may not be illegal.

> The FA Cup Final is a similar example, where prices are kept low to reward the true fan. How many other such instances can you think of?

1.3 Price set too high: development of a surplus

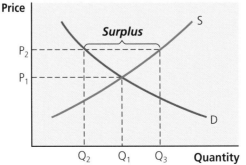

Figure 1.27

For a price to be set too high, it will usually involve a third party. The most obvious example is when government gets involved in the agricultural industry. In order to stabilise farm income, prices are sometimes fixed too high. Surpluses develop, as illustrated in Figure 1.27. This can lead to problems, as we will see when we look at the Common Agricultural Policy in Unit 4.

1.4 Maximum and minimum pricing

It is important to note the difference between the effect on the market of a price which is fixed too high or too low, as opposed to a maximum or minimum price.

A maximum or minimum price only distorts the market on one side of the equilibrium.

If a **maximum price** is set **below** equilibrium, it will distort the market and cause a **shortage**. If it is **above** market equilibrium, then it will have **no effect** on the market.

If a **minimum price** is set **above** equilibrium, it will distort the market and cause a **surplus**. If it is **below** market equilibrium, then it will have **no effect** on the market.

> It is common to make the mistake of responding to a question by saying that maximum or minimum distorts either side of the equilibrium.

1.5 Variable supply and the use of buffer stocks

Because demand and supply are relatively inelastic for many commodities, small changes in the supply function can produce significant price volatility. One policy is to stabilise prices with the use of buffer stocks, as illustrated in Figure 1.28.

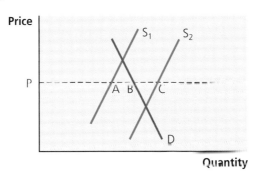

Figure 1.28

S_1 and S_2 represent the limits to output variability. In order to stabilise the price at P, when output is high, at point C, the difference between B and C will have to be purchased and placed in stock. When output is low, at point A, then the difference between A and B can be released from stock. In theory this will stabilise prices, but in practice there are potential problems:

- The range of variability may not be known.
- Administration costs might be high.
- Storage costs might be high.
- There may be a tendency for the price to be set too high and overproduction to prevail.
- Many producers, who may be in different countries, are required not to abuse the system.

2 *More failure than imperfection*

2.1 Introduction

Often in economics market imperfection is taken to mean a failure as the market is not working perfectly. However, there is a difference between markets that allocate resources inefficiently because of imperfections as opposed to failing to allocate resources at all.

2.2 The rationale behind economic intervention in a market economy

2.2a Introduction

Academics that study political economy argue a case for the mixed economy based upon the observation of weaknesses at both extremes. The argument for intervention by government is associated with the identification of various types of economic good. These have degrees of imperfection and the potential to fail if left to the free market. These economic goods range from:

- the **pure public good** to
- the **pure private good**

> Without some degree of government intervention, there would be anarchy, where resources would be allocated by the laws of the jungle.

2.2b Types of economic good

Pure public good

A pure public good is necessarily collectively consumed. It is **non-rival** and **non-excludable**. If one person has it, the whole group can have it. If any producer provides it for one consumer, it is provided for all other members of the group. The often-quoted examples are street lighting, water purification, prevention of contagious disease, law and order and internal and external defence. The fact that individuals will not buy the product is an economic justification for taxation and collective demand, but does not necessarily mean that the product should be produced by the state.

> A common mistake by students is to include education and health as public goods because they are paid for out of the public purse.

Quasi-public good

A quasi-public good is something that is likely to have started as a public good, usually because property rights have not been recognised or, if recognised, have not been enforced. This means that it has the potential to become a private good. For example, a beach could be fenced off and made excludable.

Pure private good

If a pure private good is consumed by one person, it cannot be consumed by anyone else; and if provided for one person, it cannot be provided for anyone else. Therefore it is **rival** and **excludable**. Examples include food and clothing.

> Arguably, some forms of clothing are not pure private goods as they are worn to have an effect on other people.

Club goods

These are public goods inside an organised group which are private with respect to people outside the group. The cinema and the discotheque are rival and excludable to those outside but non-rival and non-excludable to those inside.

Merit goods

These are private goods, but they are **under-consumed** as a result of market imperfections. Arguably, in order to benefit society, the government needs

This point is arguable because many countries do not recognise the need to intervene.

to become involved in the supply and/or demand for these products. The most commonly-quoted examples are the National Health Service and state education. It is generally agreed that these products should be substituted to increase consumption.

Demerit goods

These are also private goods, but they are **over-consumed** as a result of market imperfections. Arguably, government can benefit society by restricting the consumption of these products. This can be achieved through indirect taxation. Examples include smoking, drinking alcohol and gambling. It is interesting to ask the question: how would government manage without the revenue from these three products if people really did give them up?

Be warned: it is a common error to think of social costs and externalities as the same thing.

2.2c Externalities

- Private costs or benefits + external costs or benefits = social (total) costs or benefits.

The extent to which there are externalities is used to justify government intervention. This will be looked at in more detail later in these revision notes.

Externalities are market imperfections that can occur as the result of either **production or consumption**. For example, if a firm discharges waste into a local river and kills the fish, this is an external cost. If it discharges a waste product that feeds the fish and improves local fishing, this is an external benefit. External costs are similarly referred to as negative externalities, while external benefits are positive externalities. Also, externalities are often referred to as **spillover** effects on third parties. There is never a contract to pay for external costs or benefits. If there is, then they are no longer external but are internalised and become private costs or benefits.

2.2d Information failure

Information failure occurs when producers and/or consumers do not have perfect information. Individual consumers may over- or under-consume goods. They may find the information provided about a good too complicated to understand or they may find a valuation of future benefits difficult. In such markets intermediaries such as financial advisers may be used to fill the information gap, but even professionals cannot predict precisely future events, such as stock market valuations. Normative statements are made which require individual value judgments and these may differ from one person to another.

It is agreed by economists that without government intervention, information failure would lead to the under-consumption of merit goods such as health and education. This is because the current and future benefits of the good are normally undervalued by individuals. Information failure also leads to demerit goods such as alcohol, gambling and junk food being overvalued and over-consumed.

2.2e Immobility

In perfect markets all products and productive factors would be perfectly mobile. In reality, product distribution is slowed down by 'red tape' and national boundaries, while productive factors — particularly labour — does not always make an efficient and immediate response to changing market conditions.

The older people become, the harder it is to learn new skills, while people often choose to stay in one location rather than move to a new location where jobs may be plentiful and incomes higher. To a greater and lesser degree labour is:

- occupationally immobile
- geographically immobile

3 Government intervention in the supply of goods and services

3.1 Nationalised industries

Although there are fewer and fewer nationalised industries, their products have been supplied under near-monopoly conditions and their prices have often been influenced by political rather than economic circumstances.

3.2 The effect of taxation and expenditure

Expenditure taxes like VAT and excise duties change prices. These changes can be significant as in the case of **demerit goods** like alcohol and cigarettes as well as fossil fuels, particularly petroleum.

By collectivising demand, the government changes the pattern of demand from what it would be in a free market. This is obvious in the case of **public goods** which are collectively demanded as they are unlikely to be provided in a free market. If **merit goods** are provided free to the consumer, markets will be distorted.

There are not many countries which provide merit goods like health and education free to the consumer.

3.3 Government control over the supply of goods free to the consumer

3.3a The case for providing products free to the consumer

- **Public goods:** there is a strong case for supplying these **collective consumption goods** free to the consumer. Law and order and defence will be demanded collectively, but not individually because they are **non-excludable**. There is almost universal agreement among economists that taxes should be raised to finance the demand for public goods.
- **Merit goods:** the case for merit goods is not as strong. This is because **health** and **education** are **private goods** which would be traded in a marketplace. The argument which supports intervention is that these products will be under-consumed when **externalities** are taken into account.

Would all parents be prepared to pay the necessary amounts on educating their children up to the level required to benefit society?

Arguably, health and education provide external benefits to society as well as private benefits to individuals. Expenditure on these products can be considered an **investment in human capital**.

Not to be confused with the free good, e.g. air or sun.

3.3b The case against providing products free to the consumer

The case against supplying the consumer with goods free is one of non-optimal allocation of scarce resources. If consumers maximise utility, they will consume the 'free' good up to the point where marginal utility is zero. At this point

the marginal cost of producing the last unit is likely to be relatively high and certainly higher than zero. This will bring about inefficiency because scarce resources will have been used in order to produce products that will give rise to very low additional utility.

If we assume **no externalities**, then a price charged for these merit goods will reduce consumption and release resources to produce products which have a higher marginal utility. Therefore the **total utility** received by households will be lower if merit goods are provided free and higher if offered at a price.

However, if we assume externalities which are benefits, then the issue becomes one of providing the products either **free** or at a **subsidised price**.

The argument hinges upon the elasticity of demand for the product. If demand is elastic between the subsidised price and zero, then more resources will be wasted (see Figure 1.29(a) where MC_1 is much higher at Q_2 than in Figure 1.29(b), where the elasticity is lower and fewer resources will be wasted).

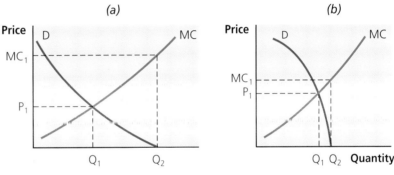

Figure 1.29

The case for providing certain goods free is based upon the **imperfections** of the marketplace and the implicit assumption that governments can produce a more efficient allocation of resources. This assumption has been questioned by a number of economists who argue that the **inefficiencies of government** far outweigh the inefficiencies of the marketplace.

A final point is that government intervention costs money whereas the marketplace does its job with no charge.

4 An introduction to welfare economics

4.1 Total costs and total benefits

Arguably all or almost all products give rise to externalities and these complicate the theories of optimality and efficiency. The divergence between the private costs and social (total) costs of production and the private benefits and social (total) benefits from consumption are referred to as **market imperfections**.

In order to make decisions, it is useful to complete a **cost–benefit analysis**, where total costs and benefits are measured. It is the task of cost–benefit analysis to estimate all costs and benefits in money terms. Private costs and benefits are relatively easy to measure. Unfortunately, external costs and benefits are

difficult to measure. If total costs are less than total benefits, a certain type of resource allocation will benefit society, even though private costs may have been greater than private benefits. In this case resource allocation would have produced losses in a private market.

Some economists have suggested that almost any cost–benefit analysis can produce a positive or negative answer. It all depends upon what is included in (or excluded from) the analysis, and the money values given to intangibles like human life and the preservation of the countryside.

> This is a good critical point to bring out in essays.

4.2 Positive and normative statements

Welfare economics highlights the importance of identifying the difference between the terms positive and normative. A positive statement usually includes **'was'**, **'is'** or **'will be'**, whereas a normative statement usually includes **'ought'**, **'should'** or **'must be'**.

A positive statement is likely to be made by an economist to describe an actual or probable event, whereas a normative statement is a subjective value judgement that is more likely to be made by a politician.

4.3 Different points of view

- Welfare economists envisage an important role for government in correcting market failure.
- Free market economists cast doubt on the ability of government to acquire the knowledge necessary to improve upon the market. They would like to limit the government role to easing the entry of firms, products and productive factors into the marketplace, through the clarification of private property rights and the creation of a level playing field of rules and regulations which promote fair competition.

> The degree of government intervention is a fundamental argument which has shifted throughout this century and the twentieth century. Traditionally, Tories are associated with free markets and Labour with intervention. However, the reality is that some Tory governments have supported intervention while some Labour governments have encouraged free markets.

Government success or failure?

In allocating resources more efficiently, governments may be considered successful when they:

- promote public goods
- increase consumption of merit goods
- manage external costs and benefits
- provide information
- prevent market dominance
- encourage greater equity

or they may be considered a failure when they:

- develop unnecessary bureaucracy
- do not have the information to improve on the market
- misjudge costs and benefits
- provide the wrong information
- abuse their dominant position
- waste money and misallocate resources

A The circular flow of income and how it is measured

1 Introducing the circular flow of income

In the UK income is measured using money that flows through the economy between consumers and producers. This process is continuous and the same money is used again and again to create income. In a short space of time, the same money may be passed from consumer to producer in payment for a product and from producer to productive factor in payment for a service.

The smooth flow of income can be interrupted in several ways:

- Consumers and producers can temporarily withdraw money from the circular flow. However, saved money has a price (the rate of interest) and this may encourage the surplus money to be placed with a financial intermediary who can recycle it to other consumers who need to borrow or producers who want to invest.
- Government may take away some of the income in the form of tax which they return to the economy when they spend on behalf of their citizens.
- Money may flow out of the economy if producers and/or consumers make purchases in foreign countries while foreigners purchasing goods and services in the UK add income to the UK economy.

As a result of the above, macroeconomic models may be:

- simple two-sector models, where producers and consumers buy and sell as well as save and invest
- a closed model, where government taxation and expenditure is added
- an open model, where imports and exports are included

2 Important definitions

These are just a few of the main terms used in measuring national income.

All of the aggregates are calculated over specific time periods, often 1 year.

Property refers to the ownership of a wide range of assets, i.e. land, buildings, shares, government securities.

Gross national income: the sum total of income received by the factors of production i.e. wages + profits + interest + rent.

(Net) national income: gross national income minus depreciation of capital stock at factor cost (see below). The net is in brackets to remind you that reference to national income is always net national income, not gross national income.

Gross domestic product (GDP): the total value of all domestically produced goods and services.

Gross national product (GNP): GDP plus property income from abroad minus property income paid abroad.

Net national product: GNP minus depreciation of capital stock.

Total final expenditure: the total expenditure on domestic products by UK and foreign residents. Aggregate expenditure can be subdivided into:

- consumer expenditure
- government expenditure
- capital expenditure
- stockbuilding
- exports

All the above can be measured at:

Market price which includes indirect taxes but excludes subsidies.

Factor cost which excludes indirect taxes but includes subsidies.

This measure is used to show changes in output as it is adjusted for any price changes.

Constant prices which shows the value of output for each year in terms of the prices ruling in a base year.

3 National income

3.1 Measurement and its problems

Over a specific period of time the national income can be measured by adding up the value of its:

- **output**
- **income**
- **expenditure**

All three totals will be equal as they are measuring the same thing. In reality, the totals do not match exactly, so a **residual error** is indicated in the statistics. The main problems using and interpreting national income statistics are:

- **Real income:** national income statistics will need to be deflated to represent a real value:

$$\frac{\text{index number year 1}}{\text{index number year 2}} \times \text{national income year 2}$$

- **Imperfect knowledge:** not everyone tells the truth to the taxman.
- **Public goods** do not have prices.
- **Double counting** takes place unless only value added is identified at each stage in the production process.
- **DIY** products do not provide an income to be measured.
- **Externalities:** to give a true value, costs should be removed from the total while benefits are added.
- **Depreciation** is not easy to value precisely.

3.2 Using national income statistics to compare living standards

It is common in examination questions to come across the need to compare the usefulness of statistics in measuring welfare or standards of living.

3.2a Comparisons between countries

Different population sizes: national income figures are meaningless unless they are given as **per capita**.

Remember to explain that standards of living and welfare involve more than just material things. For example, being free from religious, ethnic or political persecution will raise living standards but not in a way that can be measured by national income statistics.

Different currencies: ideally **purchasing power parities** would solve this problem, but the easily available **exchange rates** do not reflect purchasing power. There are also many countries whose currencies are not freely traded on markets.

Different methods of collection: some are more comprehensive than others. The UK, for example, includes goods and services while Russia only includes goods.

Different distributions of income and wealth: the more equal the distribution, the higher is the average standard of living.

Differences in non marketed resources: climate, scenery, political stability, etc.

Differences in leisure time: if two countries produce the same income per head, then the one that does it with less working time and more leisure has the higher standard of living.

Different defence budgets: more money spent on defence means less money spent on consumer products.

Externalities: Neither costs nor benefits would be measured in national income statistics.

3.2b Comparisons over time in the same country
Population changes: statistics need to be offered in a **per capita** form.

Collection of statistics: this will change over time. In their current form, official national income statistics have only been compiled in the UK since 1941.

Changes in the value of money: throughout this century there have been inflations and deflations.

Balance of payments disequilibrium: a current account surplus depresses living standards and vice versa.

Distribution of income and wealth: this changes over time.

Changes in working conditions: improvement in non-pecuniary benefits, fewer hours worked.

Exceptional years: it would not be realistic to compare war years with other years.

Externalities: a rise in national income may be offset by a rise in external costs.

B Problems of imbalance

1 Introduction

An imbalance between the aggregate supply of products and the aggregate demand can produce problems which encourage government action.

These problems can be caused by either too much demand or too much supply.

2 The value of money

2.1 Explaining the terms

A person's money is represented by a nominal number. Its real value is the quantity of products that can be purchased with a given amount of money.

The value of money and the average level of prices are inversely related: if prices go up the value of money goes down.

Over the centuries the value of money has fallen, although during the seventeenth century it increased slightly in value. The changes in value were slow until the twentieth century when governments took control over managing money and seem to have mismanaged its value.

2.2 Measuring changes in the value of money

2.2a The difference between a change in relative prices and a change in average price

In a dynamic economy relative prices are changing all the time, but this does not necessarily mean that the average level of prices changes. A change in the value of money requires the average level to rise (inflation) or fall (deflation).

2.2b The problem of choosing representative prices

It would not be possible to measure all price changes. Therefore statisticians concentrate on **retail** prices and from these they select a **key** products basket and monitor its prices.

2.2c The use of index numbers

A lot of statistics in economics are presented in index number form. A starting date is chosen and each item is given a base value of 100.

If we assume only three products and their price change over one year, then a raw index would look like Table 2.1.

> This is important to understand. If monetarists are right, then wage rises change relative prices but they cannot change the average level of prices. Therefore, they cannot cause inflation.

> 100 is chosen so that both rises and falls keep numbers positive.

	Year 1		**Year 2**	
Product	Price	Index no.	Price	Index no.
A	5p	100	10p	200
B	15p	100	18p	120
C	100p	100	75p	75
				395

395/3 = 131.67

Table 2.1

In Year 2, prices have risen on average by 31.67%.

Problems of imbalance

2.2d The use of weights

In the previous example there is an implicit assumption that equal amounts of money are spent on each product. If this is not the case, then each product needs to be weighted to reflect its relative importance.

If we assume 50% of total consumer spending is devoted to Product A, 30% to B and 20% to C, weights can be allocated in the proportions 5:3:2. The price indices are multiplied by the weight and the average is obtained by dividing the total of these weighted indices by the **total number of weights** (not the number of products). Using the same example, we get Table 2.2.

Read this carefully — it is a common mistake to divide by the number of products.

Table 2.2

Year 1

Product	Price	Index	Weight	Weighted index
A	5p	100	5	500
B	15p	100	3	300
C	100p	100	2	200
				1000

1000/10 = 100

Year 2

Product	Price	Index	Weight	Weighted index
A	10p	200	5	1000
B	18p	120	3	360
C	75p	75	2	150
				1510

1510/10 = 151

On average, prices now show a rise of 51%. This is because the product whose price went up the most is the most heavily weighted.

Having calculated the change in the index of retail prices, it is a small step to measuring the change in the value of money. Compared to the base year, money has now fallen in value by 33.8%.

In the actual index of retail prices, key products are changed each year. Recently out are: kippers, cups and saucers, men's vests and women's stockings. Recently in are: microwave meals, bottles of mineral water, leggings and satellite television.

$$\frac{\text{base year (or previous year)}}{\text{current year}} \times 100 = \frac{100}{151} \times 100 = 66.2\% \text{ of last year's value}$$

2.3 The retail price index, the consumer price index and the harmonised index of consumer prices

Students of economics may come across:
- the retail price index (RPI), which was the traditional way of measuring price changes and was often referred to in its RPIX form, which excluded mortgage interest payments or its core rate of RPIY, which excluded mortgage interest payments, indirect taxes and council tax
- the harmonised index of consumer prices (HICP), which is the preferred way of measuring changes in the cost of living between countries of the European Union and the target measure of inflation of the European Central Bank

Some economists have suggested that the UK government chose to replace RPI, which is an arithmetic measurement with CPI, which is a geometric measurement, because geometric measures produce lower recorded rates of inflation than arithmetic measures.

There is the well-known story of how, in 1923 in Germany, a person took a barrow loaded with money to the shops. The first stop was to buy some bread and the person foolishly left the barrow load of money outside. When they came out of the shop, the barrow had been stolen. However, the money was still there. Between June and October 1923 prices rose by 5,882,352,900%.

Monetarists who believe that government is the sole cause of inflation like to point out that it is also the biggest debtor in the economy and therefore benefits by seeing a fall in the real value of the National Debt.

- the consumer price index (CPI), which is the UK version of the HICP and excludes certain volatile items such as energy and food

3 Inflation

3.1 Different types of inflation

Inflations are often described by the rate at which the **average level of prices rises**.

Creeping inflation is a few per cent a year.

Accelerating inflation is self-explanatory.

Hyperinflation ranges from hundreds to thousands to millions of per cent a year and usually leads to the downfall of the currency.

3.2 Causes of inflation

Cost-push inflation results from rises in wages, raw materials, etc.

Demand-pull inflation occurs when aggregate demand exceeds aggregate supply at full employment.

Too much money chasing too few goods: monetarists argue that all inflations at any level of employment have a monetary cause.

Imported inflation: higher prices can be imported from foreign countries.

3.3 Results of inflation

Redistribution of wealth: holders of wealth in money contracts lose, while holders of particular tangible assets gain.

Redistribution of income: some groups are better at protecting their real income so that a period of inflation produces winners and losers.

Redistribution from creditors and debtors: creditors lose as the value of their savings fall in real terms while the debtors gain as the real value of their debt falls.

Loss of business confidence: variable rates of inflation, interest, foreign exchange and profits disturb business sentiment.

Adjustment to exchange rates: usually a fall in the value of a domestic currency takes place if your rate of inflation is higher than your trading partners'.

Adjustment to living standards: as well as the redistributions already described, growth rates slow and can become negative, particularly at high rates of inflation.

Social and political disorder: high rates of inflation have, arguably, caused revolutions in South American countries and brought down governments in other parts of the world.

3.4 Some ways to control inflation

A good way to illustrate an **inflationary gap** is to use the withdrawals/injections model (Figure 2.1).

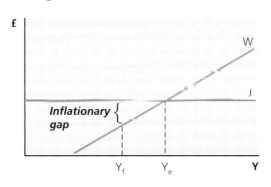

Figure 2.1

Y = national income
W = withdrawals
J = injections
Y_e = equilibrium income
Y_f = full employment equilibrium

Solutions to inflation include **reducing aggregate demand** or **increasing aggregate supply**.

In the past, **incomes policies** have been used to control wage push while some economists have argued that **unemployment should be allowed to rise** to reduce wage pressure.

Monetarists see only one solution to inflation which is to stop the money supply from growing faster than the growth in output.

Some economists accept that inflation is inevitable and therefore argue that the solution is to control the harmful redistributive effects by **index linking** mainly public sector contracts.

4 Deflation

Perhaps you could invent a word which is just the opposite of 'inflation'. When 'deflation' is taken to be the opposite of 'reflation', it means a reduction in aggregate demand irrespective of what is happening to prices. This produces a lot of potential for confusion.

4.1 Terminology

There is a problem with the term 'deflation' as it is the opposite of two words, namely Inflation and reflation. We will take it to be the opposite of inflation and therefore define it **as a fall in the average level of prices**.

4.2 The causes of deflation

Throughout history, deficient aggregate monetary demand has been caused by:
- relative shortages of monetary metal
- banking collapses
- the Wall Street Crash
- slumps in world trade

4.3 The results of deflation

Falling prices and unemployment: falling prices squeeze profits and encourage employers to shed surplus labour.

Redistribution of wealth: away from the holder of tangible assets to the holder of contracts in money.

Redistribution of income: some groups are better at protecting themselves from falls in their nominal income.

Redistribution from debtors to creditors: loan contract values increase in real terms and therefore more has to be repaid to creditors.

Loss of business confidence: profits are squeezed and difficulties occur in trying to adjust factor prices.

Adjustment to exchange rates: this time there is a rise in the value of the domestic currency unless other countries are deflating faster.

Adjustment to living standards: redistributions and a likely overall fall.

Social and political disorder: look in the history books under the Great Depression.

4.4 Some ways to control deflation

The deflationary gap is illustrated in Figure 2.2 using the withdrawals/injections model.

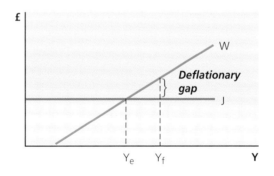

Figure 2.2

Y = national income
W = withdrawals
J   = injections
Y_e = equilibrium income
Y_f = full employment equilibrium

John Maynard Keynes had a significant influence on how policies were pursued after 1945.

The solutions to deflation can be broadly divided into **pre-Keynesian and post-Keynesian**.

Pre-Keynesian policies tended to leave factor prices to fall so that the adjustment was to the supply side of the economy.

Post-Keynesian solutions shifted the emphasis to boosting the demand side of the economy.

5 Unemployment

5.1 Important concepts

5.1a Separating unemployment from deflation

Although most definitely related to periods of deflation, unemployment has risen during periods of inflation and as the result of policies aimed at reducing the rate of inflation or disinflation.

5.1b Full employment

Under the guidance of Keynesian economists, governments used to think that they could manipulate aggregate demand to achieve and maintain full employment. Empirical evidence from the 1970s seemed to disprove this view.

5.1c A natural level of unemployment

Other economists believe that when prices are stable, any economy will settle at a level of unemployment which is determined by market forces and a range of institutional factors. The percentage of the workforce unemployed will vary from country to country and from time to time in the same country. These differences occur as the result of changes on the supply side of the economy. In the view of these economists, no amount of demand management can have any long-term effect on the natural level of unemployment.

These may be legal, political or cultural.

This level is now commonly referred to as the non-accelerating inflation rate of unemployment (NAIRU).

5.2 Types of unemployment

Unemployed people are not part of a homogeneous grouping and economists have identified a number of distinct types:

- **casual:** irregular work, e.g. affected by weather
- **cyclical:** brought about by recession and depression in the trade cycle
- **disguised:** people are unemployed but there are no records
- **export:** decline in export markets
- **frictional:** said to exist when jobs are available in one area and people are unemployed in another
- **regional:** related to a particular part of the country
- **seasonal:** related to seasonal changes in climate
- **structural:** related to the decline of a major industry
- **technical:** capital replacing labour
- **unemployable:** physically or mentally unable to work
- **voluntary:** chosen to and is able to live without work

The fact that there are many types suggests that there cannot be one solution to the unemployment problem.

5.3 Causes and solutions to unemployment

If unemployment is judged to be **demand deficient**, then boosting demand by budgeting for a deficit and lowering interest rates may be the solution.

Structural unemployment may require retraining and increased labour mobility.

Frictional unemployment requires improvements in mobility.

Supply-side restrictions may be distorting labour markets. Freeing these restrictions is the solution.

A short-term solution to unemployment caused by imports may be protection through **tariffs and quotas**.

Fixed currencies can cause a problem if they become overvalued. Devaluation or controlled depreciation may be a solution.

The poverty trap captures a number of people who judge there is no financial advantage to work. A solution may be **reverse income tax**.

5.4 Is there a relationship between price stability and the level of employment?

5.4a Phillips thought there was

From empirical evidence, A. W. Phillips established a relationship between the level of employment and the rate of change of wages. From this model a theoretical inverse relationship between inflation and unemployment was established and this underpinned government policy during the 1960s and 1970s.

Figure 2.3
The Phillips curve

The model shown in Figure 2.3 predicts that above a certain level of employment, inflation will start to rise, whereas below a certain level, deflation will occur.

This opinion was voiced in a paper written by M. Friedman entitled 'Inflation and unemployment' for the 1976 Nobel Memorial Lecture.

5.4b Friedman was not so sure

The Phillips curve does not predict what happened during the 1970s when both unemployment and inflation rose together. Some economists had their doubts about the model and M. Friedman suggested that although there may be some short-term relationship between higher levels of employment and **unanticipated** inflation, over the long term, the relationship was not as predicted. In fact, he suggested that both inflation and deflation had distorting effects on markets and could cause unemployment to rise.

6 *Imbalance on the current account of the balance of payments*

Wherever the word 'balance' appears on accounts it is referring strictly to the difference between two totals.

The balance of payments shows how the UK economy has interacted with the other trading nations of the world. It is an account that identifies the difference between the total payments into and out of a country, measured in domestic currency over a given period of time. The balance of payments is comprised of three significant components:

- The **current account**, which is the difference between the value of exported and imported goods and services, and income flows generated from the ownership of foreign assets, foreign aid and other current transfers.

- The **capital account**, which includes transfers in the ownership of fixed assets.
- The **financial account**, which comprises transactions in financial assets and liabilities such as the ownership of UK shares by foreigners or the purchase of foreign holiday homes by UK citizens.

Of these three accounts, by far the most important measure of a nation's financial health is what happens on the current account.

- A current balance deficit means that consumers in the UK are spending more money on foreign products than foreigners are spending on UK products. This has implications for domestic employment and the exchange rate, which is considered overvalued.
- A current balance surplus means that the UK is spending less on foreign products than foreigners are spending on UK products. This has implications for domestic consumption and the exchange rate, which is considered undervalued.
- A current balance equilibrium exists when, over a period of months, the deficits on the current account are broadly matched by the surpluses.

Over the last 50 years deficits on the UK current account have exceeded surpluses by the monthly account and by value such that UK citizens have been consuming more foreign products by value than they have sold to foreigners. These consumption advantages have been offset by continual pressure on the exchange rate to devalue when it is fixed and depreciate when it is floating against foreign currencies.

C Problems of instability

1 Introduction

Over time, economists have noticed fluctuations in economic activity, some more regular than others. An obvious example is the **trade cycle**.

Also over time, the peaks appear a little higher than last time and the troughs are not quite so low; in other words, the economy is growing. It may be that **economic growth** creates instability or that the instability fuels economic growth.

2 Fluctuations in economic activity

2.1 The trade cycle

2.1a Phases

Depression: the economy is characterised by high unemployment, stable or falling prices, profits and incomes.

Recovery: this sometimes starts in the capital goods sector. Demand rises, jobs are created, profits and incomes start to rise.

Boom: full employment, rising prices and profits.

Recession: profits and incomes are squeezed and unemployment begins to rise.

2.1b Irregular fluctuations

The trade cycle is often associated with the nineteenth century. The twentieth century has been much more irregular and theorists tend to talk of fluctuations in economic activity in terms of **cumulative movements** where momentum builds up. The multiplier and accelerator fit in here. Then there are **highs and lows** from which a reversal of direction or a **turning point** is recorded.

Economists who try to predict the future are interested in cycles. The **Kondratief cycle** is spread over a period of 50 years whereas business cycles can be played out in less than 10 years.

2.1c Theories of cyclical events

Under-production or over-consumption may cause the economy to reverse direction.

Business confidence may be jolted by real events; or rumours and uncertainties about the future may lead to a 'lemming' response.

Keynesians have their own theories related to the multiplier and accelerator.

Monetarists refer to supplies of money growing at rates which are different to output.

3 Economic growth

3.1 What is economic growth?

One definition of economic growth is **an increase in the productive capacity per capita over time**. This is clearly distinct from a growth in output due to the

> Not to be taken too seriously, but the American president Harry S. Truman said: 'It's a recession when your neighbour loses his job; it's a depression when you lose yours.'

increased use of existing capacity. Figure 2.4 shows the movement from X to Y as increased use of existing capacity while the production possibility boundary shifting outwards from AB to A_1B_1 is economic growth.

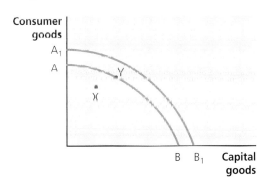

Figure 2.4
Production possibility
boundaries

3.2 Why is economic growth desirable?

Over the next 45 years, if the world economy grows at only 2.5% per annum on average, its citizens will be three times better off than they are today.

Economic growth offers the prospect of reducing poverty without having to make some people worse off.

Economic growth allows people to increase their leisure time and their standard of living.

People have come to expect rising living standards and economic growth can fulfil all expectations.

3.3 Sources of economic growth

> Innovation is the role of the entrepreneur but, arguably, the single most important source of economic growth throughout history is invention.

There are various sources of economic growth:
- invention and innovation
- improvements in the quality of labour
- investment in capital stock
- increased mobility of productive factors
- more efficient allocation of resources
- moving from small- to large-scale production
- capitalism and the profit motive

3.4 The costs of economic growth

> Link section 3.2 to section 3.4 and you have an answer to questions about the costs and benefits of economic growth.

The **opportunity cost** of resources allocated to economic growth is foregone consumption and lower living standards in the present.

The **social costs** of economic growth are described in many forms, e.g. rising incomes lead to more cars, more pollution and more congestion.

The **personal costs** of economic growth are that people need to be occupationally and geographically more mobile. This leads to disruption and unpleasant breaks in working life.

3.5 Are there limits to economic growth?

3.5a The doomsday case

Some economists predict a growth-induced doomsday brought about by pressure on natural resources. It will result from:

- accelerating population growth
- a worldwide desire to raise living standards
- exhaustion of non-renewable resources within the next 50 years satisfying accelerating demand throughout the world
- damage to the ozone layer
- global warming
- flooding of low-lying areas
- increased pollution of the atmosphere, rivers and seas

 As these are not likely to be forthcoming, the result will be doomsday later this century.

Solutions involve:
- cutting back on use of natural resources
- reducing investment
- cleaning up the environment
- cutting the birth rate

3.5b A reply to doomsday

Mistakenly, the doomsday case is based upon weak assumptions including:
- no technical progress
- no new resources discovered
- no old resources rendered usable by new techniques
- no substitution of non-renewable resources by renewable resources
- accelerating population growth

The other economists argue for technical developments, a world that can afford to clean up the environment and a **price mechanism** that will ensure that, as resources become scarce, prices will rise and make it profitable to utilise other resources and search for substitutes.

Who has seriously considered this possibility?

A final point often ignored by the scientists is that the **benefits** from global warming may far outweigh the **costs**.

3.6 Sustainable economic growth

If we conclude that economic growth is desirable, then it is most likely we will agree that the growth must be sustainable, so that current consumption of products does not compromise the living standards of future generations. There is no doubt that since the turn of the Millennium, China has been growing faster than it has grown before and faster than most other countries. However, the question has been asked: is this sustainable growth? Non-renewable coal resources have fuelled much of the growth and brought with it more air pollution and the associated manufacturing has increased water pollution. As cars replace bikes, low emission standards have made cities like Beijing polluted up to the point of being a concern to the Olympic Committee that athletes' health may be at risk. Throughout the world, levels of concern have been raised about environmental degradation, including:

 One suggestion is to ban cars in Beijing for several days before the Olympics in order to clear the air.

- overfishing
- deforestation
- reduction in biodiversity
- land exhaustion
- air, river and sea pollution

D Government and the economy

1 Government's role

The role of government is to:

They need not necessarily be supplied by the state.

- **provide public goods:** there is almost universal agreement among economists that non-rival, non-excludable products must be bought by the state.
- **provide merit goods:** there is much debate as to whether health and education should be provided free, should be subsidised or should be left to the marketplace.
- **provide social security:** there is much debate about the level and way in which social security payments are made.
- **provide a legal framework to the economy:** this covers monopolies, mergers, restrictive practices, fair trade, factory acts, public health, etc.
- **influence resource allocation** of merit and demerit goods, imports and exports, capital goods and consumer goods.
- **regulate the overall level of economic activity** using fiscal and monetary policy.

2 Public finance and the budget

2.1 Once a year

Under normal circumstances, the Chancellor of the Exchequer presents his annual budget to Parliament. It will review the past year and set out or reinforce guidelines for the future.

The budget can be analysed on two levels: first, it is how government expenditure is financed; and, second, it is how the budget is used to manage economic policy. Using the budget in this way is referred to as carrying out **fiscal policy**.

2.2 Government expenditure

A large proportion of national income is spent, on your behalf, by the government. We have identified the need for spending on **public goods**, but much other spending by government is the basis for academic debate. The difficulty is how much government spending is necessary to promote an **optimum allocation of resources**.

In any year, the government is concerned with maintaining the **current** level of service as well as changing, adding and improving, which involves **capital** spending.

The pattern of government expenditure involves direct expenditure on products, including public and merit goods, transfer payments as part of its welfare commitment, and servicing the National Debt.

2.3 Taxation

2.3a Economists and taxes

Economists investigate the tax system in terms of its effect on **efficiency**. Questions of fairness, equity and justice are not the direct concern of economists. What is important is whether a tax produces a more or less efficient allocation of resources.

An economist may look at the likely impact of a number of taxes, all of which will bring about a less efficient allocation of resources but a more equitable distribution of income and wealth.

If the issue is between direct and indirect taxes or proportional and progressive taxes, then questions must be asked about their effect on the incentive to work, invest, save, or even stay in the country. And how will the tax affect demand, prices and employment?

In principle, taxes are based upon the following four canons:
- equity
- certainty
- economy
- convenience

Economists encouraged government to drop high marginal income tax rates as some estimates suggested they cost more to administer than the revenue they raised.

2.3b The structure of taxes

Progressive taxes are where higher income earners pay proportionally more of their income in tax.

Proportional taxes are where the same proportion of income is paid in tax by the different income groups.

Regressive taxes are where the lower income earners pay a higher proportion of their income in tax, and the higher income earners pay a lower proportion in tax.

2.3c Direct taxation

These taxes are paid to the **Inland Revenue**. They are levied on income and wealth and the burden of tax cannot be shared.
The main taxes are:
- income tax
- corporation tax
- petroleum taxes
- capital gains tax
- inheritance tax
- stamp duties

Food for thought — G. Gilder wrote that 'highly progressive tax rates do not redistribute incomes, they redistribute taxpayers'.

The advantages of income tax:
- progressive and redistributive
- large tax take
- PAYE is difficult to evade
- fairly precise estimates

The disadvantages of income tax:
- disincentive to work, particularly with high marginal rates of tax

Tax evasion is illegal
while tax avoidance is
legal.

- tax evasion among non-PAYE group
- resources wasted trying to avoid tax
- may reduce the potential savings of high income earners
- may encourage high earners to emigrate

The advantages of corporation tax:
- reduces potential dividends to high income earners
- does not affect costs, prices and resource allocation

The disadvantages of corporation tax:
- reduces profits and may discourage enterprise
- can be avoided by multinational companies

2.3d Indirect taxation

These taxes are paid to **Customs and Excise**. They are **expenditure taxes** and the burden can be shared between producer and consumer.

The main taxes are:
- VAT
- excise duties
- car tax
- tariffs
- miscellaneous licences

Quite a few so-called
tax havens, which
attract high income
earners, have very high
expenditure taxes.

The advantages of indirect taxes are that they:
- can be used to discourage consumption, e.g. demerit goods, non-renewable resources
- can raise a large amount of revenue quickly
- are difficult to evade
- are relatively simple to collect
- do not make taxpayers feel forced to pay them
- can be used to manage the balance of payments current account

The disadvantages of indirect taxes are that:
- they place a heavier burden on the poor because of their regressive nature
- differential rates are usually limited to products with inelastic demand curves
- they raise the cost of living and may affect inflation
- they could cause jobs to be lost

2.3e Some often asked questions

What effect do changes in expenditure taxes have on prices?
This depends mainly on the elasticity of demand for the product. Perfectly inelastic demand leads to the price rising by the amount of the tax (Figure 2.5), whereas perfectly elastic demand leads to no price change (Figure 2.6).

With a normal downward-sloping demand curve, the **tax incidence** will be shared between producer and consumer (Figure 2.7).

The producer pays a greater proportion of the tax if the demand curve is **elastic**, while the consumer pays the largest proportion if the curve is **inelastic**.

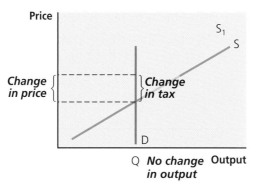

Figure 2.5

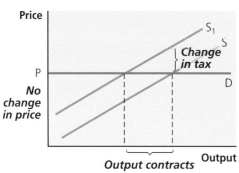

Figure 2.6

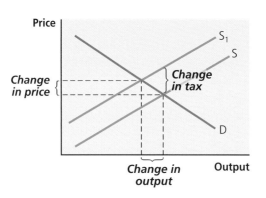

Figure 2.7

This means you can take away income and there is still more flowing through the system.

Why not tax wealth rather than income?

Wealth is very unevenly distributed compared with income, so it has been argued that the whole foundation of taxation should be changed from income to wealth.

There are a number of problems in using wealth:
- the source of wealth is difficult to distinguish
- it could create a disincentive to accumulate capital
- it could lead to fragmentation of businesses and loss of economies of scale
- income is a stream, but wealth is a stock and therefore the source can be destroyed by the tax

These people have been recorded as paying the highest implied marginal rate of tax on income.

Will negative (reverse) income tax help remove the poverty trap?

The poverty trap exists because people start paying tax below the poverty line as well as receiving benefits. Therefore, there is a range of income over which a further pound earned causes them to pay tax and lose entitlement to a welfare benefit. Only a relatively large jump in income can cross this trap.

The basic idea of negative income tax is to use the current system of tax collection to offer people financial assistance.

Suppose a person starts paying income tax at £5,000 and the poverty line is £2,000, then a negative income tax of 40% will pay £2,000 to a person who receives no income. If the person earns £1,000, he or she will be entitled to 40% of 4,000 which is £1,600, totalling £2,600.

Each time the person earns more money he or she becomes better off, which helps remove the poverty trap.

What is the relevance of the Laffer curve?

Named after Professor Arthur Laffer, the Laffer curve has important implications for political decisions.

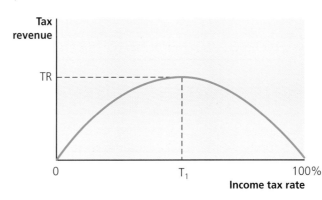

Figure 2.8
The Laffer curve

Laffer suggested that as the income tax rate rises, so the tax take will increase up to T_1 where maximum revenue will be achieved (Figure 2.8). After T_1, revenue will fall as tax rates rise.

> This is and has been a vote winner for governments in the UK and US.

Laffer suggested that many large government, high-tax countries had raised rates above T_1. There was thus scope to **lower tax rates** and **raise tax revenue**.

What are the advantages of taxing demerit goods and subsidising merit goods?

An indirect tax on demerit goods will raise the price and reduce the consumption of a product to reflect its external **cost** to society (Figure 2.9).

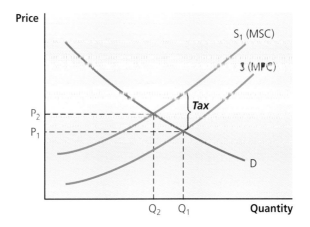

Figure 2.9
Demerit good

MSC = marginal social cost
MPC = marginal private cost

A subsidy on a merit good will lower the price and increase the consumption of a product to reflect its external **benefits** to society (Figure 2.10).

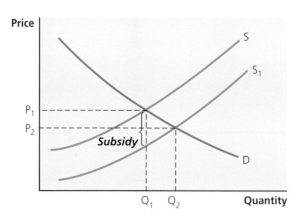

Figure 2.10
Merit good

3 Borrowing and the National Debt

3.1 The PSBR/PSDR and the National Debt

In pursuit of fiscal policy the government may produce a deficit budget, in which case it will require a **public sector borrowing requirement**. If it achieves a budget surplus, it may make a **public sector debt repayment**.

These year-on-year debts and surpluses change the nominal size of the **National Debt**.

> This debt has been with us since the Bank of England was set up in 1694 by William III. By the end of his reign the debt was £49 million.

3.2 The structure of the National Debt

The National Debt is divided into two main parts:
- traded debt
- non-traded debt

The non-traded debt includes national savings, which are held until maturity, and the traded debt includes securities that can be bought and sold on the **stock market**.

The traded debt is further subdivided into:
- short: less than 5 years
- medium: 5 to 15 years
- long: more than 15 years
- undated: with no date for redemption

Because some of the short debt, mainly **treasury bills**, are part of a commercial bank's liquid assets, the structure of the National Debt is an important element of **monetary policy**.

3.3 Financing the borrowing requirement

This is important in the **monetarist** interpretation of cause and effect.

The PSBR can be financed in a **non-inflationary** way when debt is sold to the public and spending power is transferred to government. Alternatively, debt can be financed in an **inflationary** way when government securities are left unsold at the bank and cash is printed to their value. According to the monetarists, the high inflation of the 1970s was caused by this process of money creation.

3.4 The golden rule and the stability and growth pact

Over recent years, government fiscal policy has been disciplined by the intro-duction of a 'golden rule' in the UK and adherence to the EU stability and growth pact (SGP).

The golden rule provides parameters in which fiscal policy should operate. It states that over the economic cycle the government will borrow only to invest and not to fund current expenditure. This means that over the economic cycle the budget (excluding public investment) must balance with surpluses during the boom years and deficits during the slump.

The SGP of the EU was designed to provide stability in public finance for each participating country. The UK adopted the main criteria, which are to ensure that:
● the annual budget never has a deficit of more than 3% of GDP
● national debt is to be kept at less than 60% of GDP

The members of the EU have found it difficult to adhere to these rules and most recently both France and Germany stepped outside the limits, arguing that the rules are too inflexible, particularly over the downturn in an economic cycle.

4 *Introducing fiscal policy*

After the Second World War, John Maynard Keynes persuaded governments that they could use their budgetary policy in a way that could stabilise the economy at a level of full employment.

Before the war, budgets were like any household budget. If the government wanted to spend more money, then it would raise more taxes, and if it decided to cut taxes then it would have to reduce expenditure.

Keynes explained that any capitalist economy had a tendency to progress through a cycle of economic states ranging from a recession to a depression and then through recovery to a boom. This economic cycle was exacerbated by government budgets, which were a significant part of aggregate demand.
● During the economic downturn, governments received fewer taxes and spent less money, reinforcing the weakening of economic activity
● During the economic upturn, governments received more taxes and spent more money. This was likened to a central heating system without a thermostat, as the economy was now likely to overheat

Keynes pointed out that governments should work in a counter-cyclical way using their budget to manage the overall level of aggregate demand and maintain a high level of employment. This became known as fiscal policy. Using the AD/AS model and assuming that the economy had a productive potential beyond which it was impossible to expand aggregate demand without causing a damaging inflation, then there are three ways in which the government can act to stabilise the economy at full employment.
● A deficit budget: if the economy was moving into a recession, then the government should boost aggregate demand by increasing expenditure and/or cutting taxes, so the aggregate demand curve shifted economic activity towards full employment, AD to AD[1] in the diagram below.

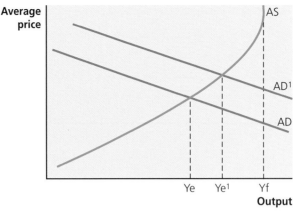

Figure 2.11

Ye/Ye¹ = equilibriums
Yf   = full employment equilibrium

- A surplus budget: if the tendency was towards a boom and what was called overfull employment (full employment with accelerating inflation), then the government should increase taxes and/or cut expenditure in order to reduce aggregate demand and inflation, AD to AD¹ in the diagram below.

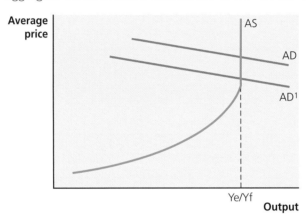

Figure 2.12

- A balanced budget: if the economy was stable at full employment, then the government should balance its budget and only spend what it had taken in taxes.

Over more recent years, this style of fiscal management has been overlooked because of its failure to deliver, particularly during the 1970s. However, there is also a political dimension to this failure. Politicians are always happy to be told to increase expenditure and cut taxes as this is vote winning. They are not so happy to be told to increase taxes and cut expenditure. This resistance meant that, since the end of the Second World War, when a roughly equal number of deficits and surpluses would have been expected to stabilise the economy, almost every year (more than 90%) there has been a budget deficit.

It is often forgotten that the supply of money is a monetary variable in its own right.

5 Introducing monetary policies

By definition, a monetary policy in the context of macroeconomic management means managing the overall level of monetary demand by making adjustments to two monetary variables:

- the supply of money
- the rate of interest

After the Second World War, when Keynesian demand management was in the ascendancy, monetary policy was subordinate to fiscal policy and was just used to accommodate fiscal targets. After Margaret Thatcher came to power in 1979, monetary policy became more important as fiscal policy was demoted to the accommodating role. Since the Bank of England was made independent in 1997, monetary targets have almost exclusively involved adjustments to the rate of interest.

Along with independence, the Bank of England was responsible for achieving an inflation target, initially set at 2.5% and measured by RPIX and later reduced to 2% and measured by CPI. If inflation fluctuates more than 1% either side of the target inflation rate, then the Governor of the Bank of England must write an open letter to the Chancellor of the Exchequer explaining why the target was missed. Operational control of monetary policy rests with the Monetary Policy Committee and they adjust the bank rate when they wish to pursue a change in the level of interest rates and aggregate monetary demand.

> The bank rate is the interest rate that is set by the Monetary Policy Committee of the Bank of England in order to influence inflation.

- Expanding the economy using monetary policy would involve lowering the repo rate. Banks would follow this by reducing their interest rates and this would encourage more borrowing. An expansion in aggregate monetary demand will shift the AD curve to the right and, depending upon the present level of economic activity, will increase either/or real output and the general level of prices.
- Contracting the economy would involve raising the bank rate and interest rates to discourage borrowing and reduce the aggregate level of monetary demand. The AD curve would shift to the left and, although the target would be to bring down the rate of inflation, there is also potential to reduce the overall level of real economic activity.

As Keynesian economists encourage the use of fiscal policy to manage the overall level of aggregate demand, so Monetarist economists argue for a particular role for monetary policy. Put simply, Monetarists argue that there should be a steady and predictable increase in aggregate monetary demand as close as possible to the rate of real growth in the economy. This will allow prices to remain stable as output expands in a growing economy.

6 | *Introducing supply-side policies*

Supply-side policies are aimed at shifting the aggregate supply curve to the right and increasing the productive capacity of the economy. Illustrated in Figure 2.13, a successful supply side policy would shift AS^1 to AS^2

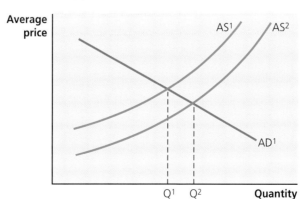

Figure 2.13

Over recent years, demand-side policies have been less concerned with promoting growth and more concerned with stabilising the economy, while supply-side policies have been actively aimed at allowing the economy to reach its full productive potential as well as promoting higher growth rates. Using a production possibility curve to illustrate a successful supply-side policy would cause a movement from inside the production possibility boundary towards the boundary, i.e. X to Y to Z. If the policy increased per capita productive capacity, it would bring about economic growth and shift the boundary outward from AB to A_1B_1.

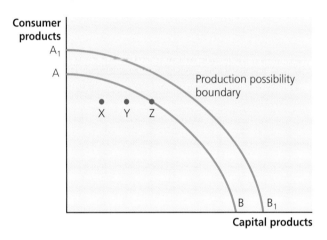

Figure 2.14

Examples of supply-side policies would be those designed to:
- improve the education and training of the workforce
- motivate the workforce
- make labour markets more flexible
- improve the distribution and communication networks
- promote competition in markets
- encourage more people to work

In order to achieve these, governments have:
- focused education and training on the development of skills
- lowered the higher marginal rates of tax
- weakened the ability of trade unions to call strikes
- privatised the telecommunications and transport networks
- imposed more restrictions on anti-competitive practices
- made it more difficult to claim unemployment benefits

There is some confusion among economists about whether certain actions by government with regard to expenditure and taxation are fiscal policy or supply-side policies. Supply-side policies include targeted government expenditure and adjustment to tax rates that may encourage rather than discourage economic activity. A simple way of dispelling this confusion is to recognise that fiscal policy involves using taxation and expenditure to change the aggregate level of demand. If expenditure and tax are changed but the overall level of aggregate demand remains unchanged, then this is a supply-side policy, not fiscal policy.

7   *Reconciling conflicts and managing macroeconomic goals*

Governments usually have four main macroeconomic policy goals. They are:

- a high level of employment
- price stability
- economic growth
- balance of payments stability

Questions are often asked about the difficulty of reconciling these targets. For example:

- Achieving a higher level of employment, particularly using demand management techniques, may aggravate inflation and cause a current account deficit on the balance of payments.
- Stabilising prices may raise unemployment and slow economic growth.
- Boosting economic growth may destabilise prices and the current account balance.
- Removing a current account deficit may reduce employment levels and growth rates.

A-level specifications usually identify four factors of production — land, labour, capital and enterprise — although some economics texts identify only land, labour and capital, preferring to consider enterprise as a component of the productive factor, labour.

Question: When does a spear become a consumer good? Answer: When it is used as a javelin.

A The factors of production

1 Definitions

- **Land** includes all natural resources, the original raw materials of production. It is important to remember that in economics the sea is land, but do not try walking on it.
- **Labour** involves all human economic effort, whether it be mental, physical, skilled or unskilled, applied to the production of goods and services.
- **Capital** is a produced means of production. The essential characteristic of capital is its quality of being able to produce more, having been produced itself. The early forms of capital were spears to kill animals, ploughs to cultivate land and nets to catch fish.
- **Enterprise** describes the factor of production which takes the risks and uncertainties of bringing together the other factors of production in the hope of a profitable return from the sale of their product.

2 Labour

2.1 Labour and population size

2.1a The dependency ratio

The dependency ratio changes over time and is different between countries. It is strictly the ratio of:

$$\frac{\text{unable to work}}{\text{able to work}}$$

Its significance is in a relatively crude observation that those who are working to produce goods and services are supporting not only themselves but also those who are not working. As the UK economy matures, so more people seem to be supported by a shrinking workforce. Whether or not this is a problem makes for an interesting debate.

Today this view is often overlooked in more developed countries, but considered much more seriously in those countries still suffering from these problems.

2.1b Are there limits to the size of a population?

The Reverend Thomas **Malthus** wrote in 1798 that the productivity of finite resources is likely to grow arithmetically (1, 2, 3, 4) while the population is likely to grow geometrically (1, 2, 4, 8). The result will be poverty, plagues, wars and starvation. These will bring back the population size to a level that the land can support.

2.1c The optimum size of a population

In theory it is quite clear:

- The optimum size of a population is that which gives rise to the highest average output for an economy.

In reality it is not quite so clear. For example, it cannot be **proved** that India is overpopulated and Australia is underpopulated. They probably are, but there is no

Do economists have a moral responsibility to point out that although countries have an optimum population size, it is not possible to identify this size in reality?

way of telling. This is an interesting point because many political debates take place on the assumption that overpopulation is proved. What is more worrying is that knowledge of the theory may encourage leaders of a country to pursue sterilisation policies or limit families to only one child. Suppose a UK government decided that unemployment was a measure of overpopulation and suggested that all people with blue eyes and blonde hair should be repatriated to Scandinavia.

Another important point to note is that optimum population size continually changes as technology changes. This means that a new invention or discovery may change a country almost overnight from being overpopulated to under-populated

2.2 The mobility of labour

2.2a The economic importance of mobile labour

It is a common error to refer to the UK as a developed economy. The UK is a developing country, as are all countries — it is just that some countries are further down the endless road than others.

In order to maintain economic development and improve efficiency, all productive factors must be sufficiently mobile to accommodate all the economic changes that take place.

Mobility not only refers to movement from place to place, i.e **geographical or lateral mobility**, but also movement from one job to another, i.e. **occupational or vertical mobility**.

Ask yourself if you would be prepared to go anywhere and do anything and then ask your parent(s) the same question.

2.2b Frictions and lateral mobility

Labour is not perfectly mobile in response to changing economic circumstances. Because the word 'labour' is a collective noun, it does not require each individual worker to be responsive to economic change. Only a proportion of the workforce needs to be mobile as economic conditions change.

A rough rule of thumb is that the faster the rate of economic growth, the more mobile the workforce needs to be to facilitate the necessary economic change.

The word 'friction' is used as it denotes the forces that stop labour moving.

2.2c Frictions and vertical mobility

If one unit of labour was a perfect substitute for another, then many frictions associated with occupational mobility would not exist.

Older members of the workforce find it more difficult to adjust to changes and to acquire new skills.

In addition, the abilities of labour are unevenly distributed. Only a limited number of people have the ability to become premier league footballers, first-rate mathematicians, linguists or steeplejacks.

2.2d Removing mobility frictions: a political dilemma

If the choice was between starvation and mobility, the workforce would be more mobile than it is today. Herein lies the dilemma: a civilised society will

want to protect its members from the genuine hardship that can come with unemployment. However, in doing this it can reinforce the frictions which slow the engine that raises living standards.

A case can also be made for the protection of certain occupations by artificial barriers:

- Do you need a degree to be a competent chartered accountant?
- Did you need to be the son of a miner to become a good miner?
- Do you need an Equity card to be a fine actor?

The question an economist must ask is whether these barriers bring about a more efficient allocation of resources or whether they do exactly the opposite and preserve unnecessarily high incomes.

> In the 1960s, the equivalent of five GCSE passes including mathematics and English was the entrance requirement for chartered accountancy.

2.3 The division of labour into specialised functions

2.3a Advantages

These are well documented in textbooks and include:

- improved dexterity
- efficient use of skills
- production line methods
- greater use of machinery

> The importance of the theory of comparative advantage will be reinforced when we look at international trade.

However, examinations usually want you to understand how division of labour allows output to expand through the **theory of comparative advantage**. In order to understand this theory it is necessary to be clear about the difference between absolute advantage and comparative advantage.

- Absolute advantage is where a productive unit, like a person, a firm or a country, can produce more output than another productive unit given the same resources.
- Comparative advantage can exist where one productive unit has an absolute disadvantage in producing all products, but has a **lower opportunity cost** of producing one or some of the products.

> This will also illustrate the theoretical basis of all trade.

The theory is best understood by following through a simple example. Suppose that over a specific period of time two people could produce the quantities of loaves of bread and pints of beer shown in Table 3.1.

Table 3.1

	Loaves of bread	Pints of beer
Geraldine	24,000	16,000
John	12,000	9,000
Total	36,000	25,000

In this example, Geraldine has **absolute** advantage in the production of both bread and beer. At first sight it would seem that specialisation would not increase total output. However, before reaching a conclusion it is necessary to apply the concept of opportunity cost. What we need to know is how much bread has to be given up to produce more beer and vice versa. Table 3.2 shows the opportunity cost of producing one loaf of bread and one pint of beer.

 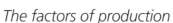
The ratios are always the reciprocal of each other.

Table 3.2

	One loaf of bread	One pint of beer
Geraldine	²/₃ pint of beer	³/₂ loaves of bread
John	³/₄ pint of beer	⁴/₃ loaves of bread

In terms of opportunity cost, John gives up fewer loaves of bread to produce a pint of beer while Geraldine gives up fewer pints of beer to produce one loaf of bread. **Comparative advantage occurs when one productive factor has a lower opportunity cost for producing one product.**

Although Geraldine has an absolute advantage in producing bread and beer, John has a comparative advantage in producing beer. If they both concentrate on the product for which they have a comparative advantage, we get the results in Table 3.3.

Table 3.3

	Loaves of bread	Pints of beer
Geraldine	48,000	0
John	0	18,000

Geraldine produces 12,000 more loaves than the previous total while John produces 7,000 fewer pints. The gain of 12,000 loaves is at an opportunity cost of 8,000 pints, but only 7,000 are lost. A loss of 7,000 pints would be at an opportunity cost of 10,500 loaves, but overall 12,000 loaves are gained. It is therefore advantageous for each to specialise.

However, so far we have not increased the total of one product without reducing the other total.

Suppose Geraldine produced only 9,000 more loaves at a cost of 6,000 pints while John produced 6,000 more pints at a cost of 8,000 fewer loaves (Table 3.4).

Table 3.4

	Loaves of bread	Pints of beer
Geraldine	33,000	10,000
John	4,000	15,000
Total	37,000	25,000

It is always possible to produce more of both products. As a bit of fun, see if you can do it.

We have proved that **when opportunity costs are different it is always possible to produce more of one product without producing less of the other product.**

A final important point is illustrated by changing the original situation very slightly (Table 3.5).

Table 3.5

	Loaves of bread	Pints of beer
Geraldine	24,000	16,000
John	12,000	8,000

A simple rule for calculating opportunity cost: if you are dealing with output, place the number on the right **over** the number on the left to get the ratio, e.g. 16,000/24,000 = $^2/_3$. If you are dealing with costs, then the number on the right goes **beneath** the number on the left.

In this situation there is no comparative advantage. You can check this by working out the opportunity costs. Do this and you will see they are the same. Play around with the numbers and you will find that it is now no longer possible to increase the output of both products. Changing one number very slightly has created a situation where there can be no advantage in specialising function. **If opportunity costs are the same, there cannot be any gains from trade.**

2.3b Disadvantages

Again, these are well documented and include:

- monotony and boredom
- a loss of craftsmanship and variety of expression
- interdependence within one firm and between firms which creates a greater risk of unemployment

The tenuous thread which binds the modern economy's productive processes is both its strength and potentially its greatest weakness.

3 Enterprise

3.1 The functions of the entrepreneur

The entrepreneur is the risk-taker who has no guaranteed rate of return. Whereas labour can insure itself against a cessation of income through ill health or redundancy, the entrepreneur takes an uninsurable risk.

It is usual for the entrepreneur to sign contracts to pay for the use of productive factors, but there is no contract with the consumer that can guarantee profits.

3.2 The decision of optimum factor combination

The successful entrepreneur will find the most efficient mix of productive factors. This decision is illustrated using Figure 3.1.

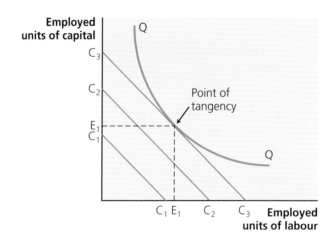

Figure 3.1

Although this is the most efficient combination, it does not tell us anything about revenues and profits. It only identifies costs.

The line QQ is an isoquant. **Isoquants join together different combinations of productive factors (in this case labour and capital) which can be used to produce the same quantity of a product.** The lines C_1C_1, C_2C_2 and C_3C_3 are isocost lines.

An isocost line joins together different combinations of productive factors that can be employed for the same total cost. The point of tangency between C_3C_3 and QQ is the least cost combination of productive factors to produce a specific quantity.

The point of tangency has an algebraic formulation as it is the point where:

$$\frac{\text{marginal physical product of labour}}{\text{price of labour}} = \frac{\text{marginal physical product of capital}}{\text{price of capital}}$$

4 Land

4.1 Introduction

Land can be available for repeated use, e.g. agricultural land, or it can be used up in the production process, e.g. fossil fuels.

It is not possible to replenish many natural resources which took millions of years to form, so those **non-renewable resources** are only available for a particular use over a limited period of time. This has led to a debate between conservationists and others.

4.2 Conservation or not: the debate

4.2a Conservationists

Problem: non-renewable resources will be used up over a relatively small number of years and some renewable resources will be exhausted (for example, by overfishing and destruction of hardwood forests) if the firms and nations of the world compete for their use.

Solution: far-sighted national and international agencies must manage the controlled use of these resources.

4.2b The others

Problem: the opposing argument questions the reality of cooperation at a national and international level and even suggests that resources will be used up, without replacements coming on stream, if the market mechanism is ignored.

Solution: let the market mechanism work — shortages will lead to higher prices and profits, which will in turn encourage the search for substitutes and synthetic alternatives. Private property rights should be clearly established and resources will then be carefully farmed. As long as land remains common to all, it will be misused and exhausted.

> This leads to a difficult philosophical point, namely who should **own** the free gifts of nature if common ownership is inefficient.

4.2c Conclusion

Many economists have predicted the total exhaustion of certain raw materials. For example, the fossil fuel oil will only last for a certain number of years at current rates of consumption. In contrast, other economists have said that if the price mechanism is allowed to work, then in 500 years time there will still be huge quantities of oil unused throughout the world.

Who is right? It is your future.

5 *Capital*

5.1 Introduction

Capital can only be formed if current consumption is foregone. This means that if you want to be better off in the future, it will be necessary to lower your standard of living in the present. This has been referred to as one step back in order to take two steps forward.

5.2 Some important distinctions

All capital is wealth, but not all wealth is capital.

Capital and wealth: wealth is what you own, capital is that part of your wealth which is used to derive a flow of income. Your car is wealth — it becomes capital if you use it as a taxi.

Gross and net capital investment: capital is consumed or used up in the production process. This **depreciation** occurs through wear and tear or deterioration and can also be the result of **obsolescence** when more efficient alternatives are developed.

Gross investment is the total amount of new capital produced. **Net investment** is the total produced over and above that required to cover depreciation. For a productive unit to become more productive, net investment must be greater than zero.

5.3 The importance of capital

In all countries of the world where living standards are high, large amounts of capital per head of the population have been produced and are being used. However, **although capital investment is a necessary condition for a high standard of living, it is not sufficient on its own to guarantee economic growth.** This is particularly obvious where a country has invested large amounts in non-productive capital such as armaments.

B The size and scale of production

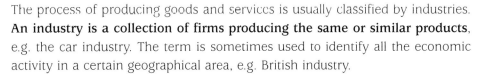

1 Introduction

1.1 Types of productive unit

It is important not to confuse the terms 'industry' and 'firm'.

The process of producing goods and services is usually classified by industries. **An industry is a collection of firms producing the same or similar products**, e.g. the car industry. The term is sometimes used to identify all the economic activity in a certain geographical area, e.g. British industry.

A firm is a legal entity distinguished from other firms by ownership. It could be as small as one person or it could be owned by thousands of shareholders, employ hundreds and thousands of people throughout the world and produce products in many different industries.

The size of the firm relative to the size of the industry is important in understanding the relationship between producer and consumer.
- many firms — competitive industry — consumer sovereignty
- one firm — monopoly — producer sovereignty

1.2 Output and time periods

Production time periods relate to the amount of time required to change output.

It is useful to identify four periods, although short run and long run are most often used in theoretical models.

- The **very short run** (momentary period) is that period of time during which it is not possible to change output.
- The **short run** allows the producer to change most of the productive factors, but at least one factor is fixed and cannot be changed.
- The **long run** allows the producer to expand or contract output by adjusting the use of all the productive factors.

In each of the above, technology has been held constant.
- In the **very long run** it is possible that technological developments can change the quality of the products or the efficiency of the productive factors.

2 In the short run

2.1 Increasing marginal returns and the law of variable proportions

This law is sometimes known as the law of diminishing marginal returns. It is important to remember that returns refers to output, not revenue or profits.

In the short run **variable** factors can be added to **fixed** factors, and it is likely through specialisation of function and division of labour that the addition to total output (marginal output) will at first rise. It is, however, not definite. What is certain, and is therefore given the status of law, is that when additional units of a variable factor are added to a fixed factor, then at some level of input of the variable factor, the addition to output will begin to diminish.

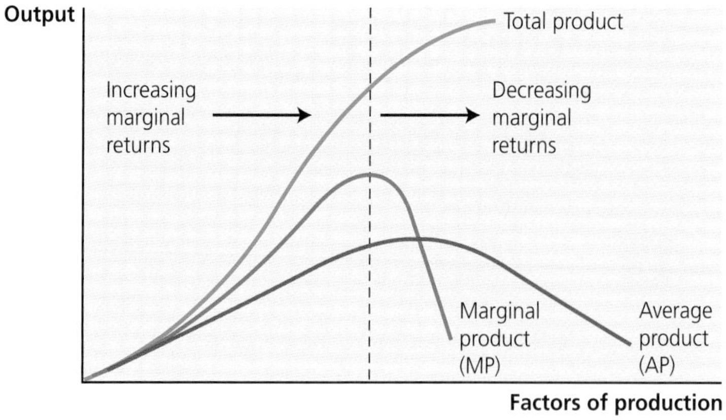

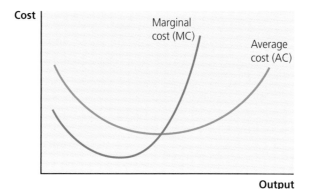

Figure 3.2

MP will always cut
AP at its highest point
after which AP will fall.

The marginal product curve in Figure 3.2 clearly illustrates the point where the law of variable proportions kicks in.

2.2 How do costs behave in the short run?

It is important to remember that the **law of variable proportions** is about **output in the short run**. However, it is obvious that it has implications for the costs of production. To illustrate this we must define two costs:

- **Fixed costs** are those costs of production which remain the same at all levels of output including zero.
- **Variable costs** are incurred as soon as the first unit is produced and subsequently vary with output.

Because fixed costs remain the same at all levels of output, they must always fall on average as output expands. If we assume that the additional costs of employing factors is constant, then falling average costs plus increasing marginal returns must bring costs down. However, as output expands, the fall in average fixed costs becomes weaker and diminishing marginal returns set in. Hence the normal shape for cost curves is as shown in Figure 3.3.

Figure 3.3

When numbers fall and
then rise, MC will cut
AC at its lowest point.

3 In the long run

3.1 A common confusion

Returns to scale should not be confused with the increasing marginal returns that occur when factor proportions vary in the short run. They occur when factor inputs are changed in the same proportion. Increasing returns to scale give rise to **economies of scale**.

Questions on economies and diseconomies of scale are popular at A-level.

3.2 Economies of scale

3.2a Internal economies of scale

Internal economies of scale result from actions taken inside the firm that reduce unit or average costs.

Capital economics include the fact that machines can be used 24 hours a day and usually refer to two principles:

- **Principle of multiples:** suppose three machines produced components for the final product. Machine A produced 40, B produced 70 and C produced 80 per time period. The least common multiple of these three numbers is 560. Therefore, to achieve maximum efficiency 14 As must be linked with 8 Bs and 7 Cs.
- **Principle of increased dimensions:** double the size of a container and the volume is increased eight times — a considerable saving in transport and storage costs.

Buying economies: bulk buying of materials can reduce the prices below those quoted to small firms.

Selling economies: the marketing and advertising budget can be spread over many more units.

Financial economies: large firms can raise loans at more favourable rates than small firms.

Managerial economies: if two firms merge, one management team takes over and the other becomes redundant.

3.2b External economies of scale

External economies of scale result from actions taken outside the firm that almost inadvertently reduce their unit costs.

Training: a firm's training budget is reduced if a local college starts offering relevant courses.

Infrastructure: a large firm setting up in an area may lead to improvements in the transportation and communication networks.

Support services: trade magazines, research units and component suppliers may be drawn towards a large firm.

3.2c Internal diseconomies of scale

Internal diseconomies of scale result from actions in the firm that raise unit costs of production.

There is an interesting debate about whether these exist only as the result of the human problem. As firms grow larger it becomes more difficult to manage, control and coordinate the workforce. This is supported by the fact that internal diseconomies do not occur in all similar firms at the same level of output. For example, Japanese workers seem much more controllable in large numbers than their UK counterparts.

3.2d External diseconomies of scale

External diseconomies of scale result from actions outside the firm that raise unit costs of production.

Productive factors are scarce. As firms and industries grow larger, so increased competition for their use can create external diseconomies, for example:

● higher wages
● higher price for raw materials
● congestion on the roads
● cost of renting space

3.3 How do costs behave in the long run?

Changing the scale of activity in the long run is likely to produce economies and diseconomies of scale, as illustrated in Figure 3.4.

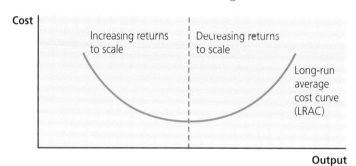

Figure 3.4

The long-run average cost curve is tangent to each of the short-run average cost curves, as shown in Figure 3.5.

Points of tangency have the same slope. Therefore as LRAC falls, so it touches SRAC where it is also falling. Only at the lowest point on LRAC will SRAC be at its lowest.

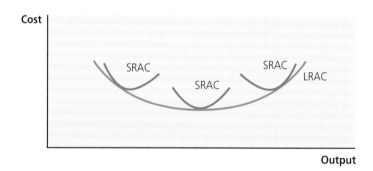

Figure .3.5

4   *In the very long run*

The main difference between the long run and the very long run is that the average costs of production can change **without** a change in output. In this case inventions, innovations, changes in technology, etc. will shift the cost curves vertically downwards, as illustrated in Figure 3.6.

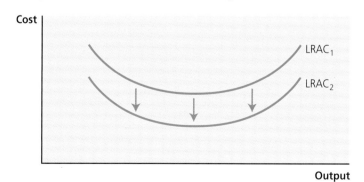

Figure 3.6

5 The optimum size of a firm

The **optimum size** of a firm is when it is producing at the **lowest point** on the average cost curve, i.e. Q_1 in Figure 3.7.

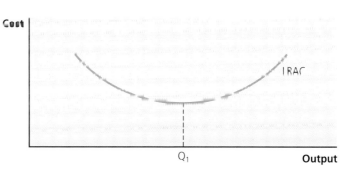

Figure 3.7

Optimum size should not be confused with optimum resource allocation which occurs when firms produce where **price** = **marginal cost** or with the most profitable output which is where **marginal cost** = **marginal revenue**.

6 The growth of firms

6.1 Why firms grow

Most economic model building of firms assumes profit maximisation as the main motivation.

- To take advantage of increasing marginal returns and returns to scale. Both of these will increase profitability.
- To increase the economic security of the firm by diversifying the product range.
- In pursuit of status, power, market dominance and the removal of actual and potential competitors.

6.2 How firms grow

Firms grow **internally** by ploughing profits back.

They grow **externally** by vertical integration, horizontal integration or by conglomeration.

How many shops in your local high street are owned by a manufacturer or product provider?

- The production process is a link between suppliers of raw materials, product providers, wholesalers, retailers and even after-sales service. If a firm takes over or merges with another firm that is at a different stage in the production process, this is described as **vertical integration**. This integration can be backwards when a product provider joins with its suppliers or forwards when it joins with the retailer.
- **Horizontal integration** is where similar firms at the same level in the production process join together.
- **Conglomeration** is where firms which are producing fundamentally different products join together, usually to produce security through diversity.

7 The small firm survives

It is common for examiners to ask why small firms survive in view of all the advantages of being large.

7.1 The demand for small firms

As incomes rise, so there is a demand for more **variety**. This is a movement away from the mass-produced, standardised product.

Quality and lasting value may be more forthcoming from a small firm.

The **limited size** of certain markets may mean it is unprofitable for a large firm with indivisible units of capital to produce at a level of output which will bring down unit costs without over-supplying the market.

Personal service may be lost in large firms but be required by customers of, for example, doctors, dentists, lawyers, accountants.

7.2 The supply of small firms

The point at which a firm reaches its optimum size will be an important factor determining its profit-maximising level of output. The degree to which firms can take advantage of economies of scale varies and this will produce different optimum sizes. Some firms may not reach optimum size until their daily production run is several hundred thousand. In contrast, firms in other industries may reach their optimum size after 50 units have been produced. Industries comprising these firms will only be profitable if they are made up of many small firms.

There seems to be no shortage of entrepreneurs willing to set up business in a small way. Small firms are more flexible. Producers do not feel so divorced from their customers and the workforce may have a greater sense of responsibility and may produce work of a higher quality.

7.3 Concluding points

7.3a Point 1

A-level questions often ask why some industries have both small and large firms, for example the UK car industry includes Ford and Morgan. In order to answer this question, segment the overall market and you will find the part supplied by Morgan will have all the characteristics of a small market.

7.3b Point 2

Up until now it has often been stated that small firms have been and will eventually be forced out of business by large firms. However, we may see the very opposite in the new millennium. Higher incomes may lead to greater demand for variety and personal service. In addition, many large firms are breaking up into smaller units as they outsource peripheral parts of the business and concentrate on their core activity.

C The theories of the firm

1 *The theory of perfect competition*

1.1 The assumptions of perfect competition

In order to build a simple model the following assumptions are well documented in textbooks:

- Industries comprise many relatively small firms.
- There are many competing consumers, i.e. there are no opportunities to form a **monopsony**.
- Products are homogeneous.
- There is perfect knowledge on the part of both producers and consumers.
- Firms have free entry into and exit from the industry.
- In the long run there is perfect productive factor mobility.
- There are no transport costs.

> An often-quoted example that comes close is the foreign exchange market which does have a homogeneous product, i.e. currency.

In real life these conditions may never apply or never apply simultaneously. It must be emphasised that the assumptions of perfect competition produce an extreme case which is primarily an analytical device to reach a certain level of basic understanding.

1.2 Important rules

1.2a Rule 1: profit maximising

> Although they are introduced here, these three rules apply to all the theories of the firm considered in this section.

It is a necessary condition for profit maximisation that output is where **marginal cost (MC) = marginal revenue (MR)**. However, it is not sufficient on its own as profits are both minimised, Q_1, and maximised at this equality, Q_2. To complete the rule, MC must be **rising** (Figure 3.8).

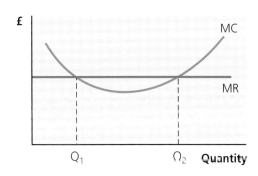

Figure 3.8

1.2b Rule 2: production in the short run

A firm will produce in the short run as long as it can cover its **variable** costs. Therefore, **total revenue is equal to or greater than total variable cost**.

1.2c Rule 3: production in the long run

In the long run a firm must produce where it can at least cover its total costs of production. Therefore, **total revenue is equal to or greater than total costs**.

The minimum required could vary from one entrepreneur to another and is therefore not a fixed amount.

1.3 Normal profits and abnormal profits

Normal profits are the minimum reward required by the entrepreneur to remain in that line of business. In economics, normal profits are considered to be a cost of enterprise and are therefore included in the costs of the firm.

Abnormal profits can include **supernormal or excessive profits** and **subnormal profits**, which are less than normal profit, i.e. less profit than that required to keep the entrepreneur in business in the long run.

1.4 The demand curve for the perfectly competitive firm

The range of output over which a firm can make a profit is such a small proportion of total output that no one firm can change output sufficiently to influence price. Each firm is then faced with a **perfectly elastic demand curve** (Figure 3.9).

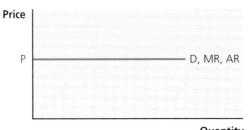

Figure 3.9

This means that the firm can sell all its products at the given market price. Therefore, the price is equal to the **marginal revenue (MR)**, which is the additional revenue from selling one more unit, and the **average revenue (AR)**, which is the price.

1.5 The supply curve for the perfectly competitive firm

A firm in perfect competition only has a **short-run supply curve**. This is because in the long run there is only one point where the firm makes normal profit. The short-run supply curve is the marginal cost above average variable cost, as illustrated in Figure 3.10.

The average variable cost curve (AVC) gets closer to the average total cost curve (ATC) as output expands. This is because the average fixed cost falls continuously as output expands.

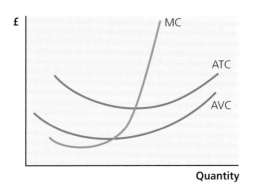

Figure 3.10

1.6 Profit-maximising output of the competitive firm

1.6a In the short run

In the short run a firm can make abnormal profits or it can minimise losses. Neither of these situations can be sustained in the long run as firms have freedom to enter or leave the industry (Figure 3.11).

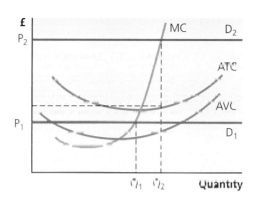

Figure 3.11

MC will cut both ATC and AVC at their lowest points.

P_1Q_1 is a loss-minimising equilibrium where firms will leave the industry. P_2Q_2 is an abnormal profit-maximising equilibrium which will attract firms into the industry. The shaded area is the area of excessive profit. For all theories of the firm, the area of excessive profit is always enclosed between the **average revenue and average cost curves**.

1.6b In the long run

When firms enter or leave the industry, then those firms already present take an increasing or decreasing share of the total market and the demand curve moves towards the long-run equilibrium where only normal profits can be made (Figure 3.12).

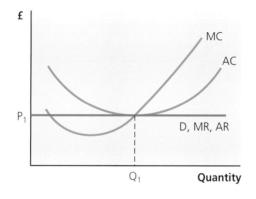

Figure 3.12

In the long run:
- All firms produce at optimum size, i.e. at the lowest point of the AC curve.
- Only normal profit can be achieved.
- Marginal cost = marginal revenue = average cost = average revenue = price.

The important equality for the entrepreneur is MC = MR, i.e. profit maximising.

1.7 Marginal and intra-marginal firms

There is a slight weakness in the argument so far in as much as all the firms in a perfectly competitive industry are identical. Should this not mean that when the industry is making a loss, all firms will, at the same time, make the decision to leave the industry?

Remember, normal profit is not a fixed amount: it is the minimum required by an entrepreneur to remain in business and this may vary from one entrepreneur to another.

For the theory to work, firms must leave the industry one after the other. To cope with this problem we can assume that the cost of enterprise varies and that only one or a few firms are in long-run equilibrium — **the marginal firms** — while other firms are making slightly more than normal profit — **the intra-marginal firms**.

1.8 Perfect competition and optimal resource allocation

Optimum resource allocation or allocative efficiency occurs when firms produce at a point where price (P) = marginal cost (MC). This means that the price the community is willing to pay for the last product is equal to the additional cost of using factor resources to produce this last product.

In perfect competition in the short and long run, P = MC.

A potential problem exists if there are external costs which are not accounted for. In this situation, price will only equal marginal private cost, not marginal social cost, and therefore **resource misallocation** will exist.

1.9 The perfectly competitive industry

1.9a The demand curve

It is often difficult to grasp how the sum of a number of horizontal demand curves for the firms can add up to produce a normal downward-sloping demand curve for the industry.

The answer is that the range over which a firm is likely to change output over the short run is considerably less than the amount required to change the market price (Figure 3.13).

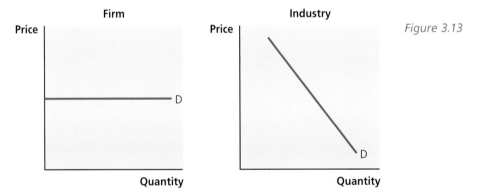

Figure 3.13

1.9b The supply curves

In the short run the firm's supply curve is the marginal cost curve above average variable cost. Therefore, in the short run the industry supply curve is an upward slope from left to right (Figure 3.14).

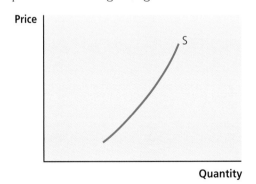

*Figure 3.14
Short-run industry
supply curve*

If we remove the constant cost assumption and have rising costs, the long-run supply curve rises from left to right or falls from left to right with falling industry costs.

In the long run, if we assume constant costs, the perfectly competitive industry supply curve is horizontal (Figure 3.15).

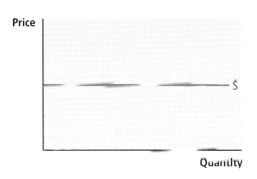

Figure 3.15
Long-run industry
supply curve

2 The theory of monopoly

2.1 Characteristics

Some textbooks refer
to perfect competition
and imperfect com-
petition, including
monopoly as an
extreme form of
imperfect competition.
Other textbooks
include all theories of
the firm which fall
between perfect
competition and
monopoly as imperfect
competition. Either
interpretation would
be accepted in
examinations.

In theory a monopoly is a single firm industry. However, in reality the UK government, through legislation, recognises that any firm which has more than a 25% share of the market is liable for investigation as a monopoly.

In theory the monopolist has complete command over the supply of a product and is referred to as a **price-maker**. However, a monopolist cannot dictate demand, but is able to discover the nature of the demand and manipulate supply to make **excessive profits**. These profits can be sustained in the long run as **barriers to entry** into the industry to prevent competing firms from entering the market.

A monopolist can **fix** either **price** or **output**, but **not both**.

2.2 The creation of barriers and the formation of monopolies

2.2a Natural barriers

Geographical distribution can produce a concentration of resources that creates a true **natural monopoly**.

Technical barriers caused by economies of scale produce monopolies which are described as natural in the sense that there are no **contrived** actions. A question which asks what market structure will develop when a firm continually benefits from increasing returns to scale is looking for the answer: a monopoly.

Local monopolies are investigated by the relevant government department and can be caused by the **transport advantages** at a particular location or the **ignorance** of potential competitors.

2.2b Deliberate barriers to exclude competition

Government has been involved in the creation of monopolies which were arguably created in the **national interest**.
- The monarchy granted firms monopoly status.
- Modern government protects a firm's invention for 16 years under the **Patent Act**.
- **Public utilities** were granted monopoly status to protect the public from exploitation.

Why have so many
public utilities been
privatised?

- Legislation to protect farm incomes has created monopolies at the level of marketing and distribution.
- **Tariffs** on imports are a source of monopoly power.
- **Quotas** provide a source of monopoly power to those firms holding a share of the quota.

In the private sector the search for increased profits encourages firms to try and become monopolies through a process of **contrived scarcity** or **anti-competitive practices**.

This may involve a number of actions to exclude competition:
- tied outlets for retailers
- subsidiary companies set up to make losses and force competitors out of the market
- persuasive advertising designed to lessen the degree of product substitutability
- mergers and takeovers

Although designed to achieve monopoly status, firms will probably have to settle for monopolistically competitive status.

2.3 Construction of the monopoly model

2.3a Preliminary considerations

The shape of the cost curves is the **same** as other theories of the firm. However, the revenue curves are **different**.

The firm is the industry and therefore the demand curve is a normal downward-sloping curve from left to right.

The **demand curve** shows how many units will be demanded at each and every price and is therefore the **average revenue curve**.

Since the price must be lowered to sell more products, the addition to total revenue, i.e. the **marginal revenue**, is less than the average revenue. This is probably easier to see using a diagram explained previously (Figure 1.12) and some new numbers (Figure 3.16).

Can you remember the elasticity of every point on the demand/average revenue curve?

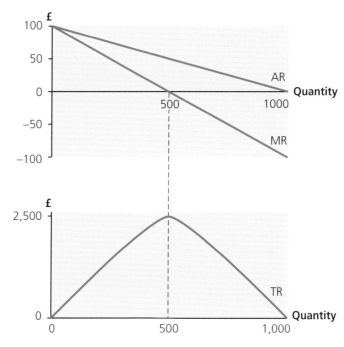

Figure 3.16
Average, marginal and total revenue curves

The simplest way to draw this diagram is to put AR and MR either side of the intersection between MC and AC. This is not a rule, as either MR or AR could intersect MC = AC, but this produces a unique rather than general case.

2.3b The equilibrium of a monopolist

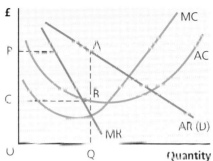

Figure 3.17

From the model in Figure 3.17, note the following points:

- The profit-maximising output is OQ where MC = MR.
- The price OP is determined by the demand curve.
- Each unit is sold for OP and costs OC to produce. Hence the rectangle, PABC, enclosed by AR and AC, is the excessive profit.
- In a monopoly there is no linear relationship between market price and quantity supplied, so there is no supply curve.
- Barriers to entry mean that the model is a long-run equilibrium.
- A distinction between short run and long run relates only to changes in the cost structure of the monopolist.

2.3c Monopoly and non-optimal resource allocation

The rule for an optimum allocation of resources is P = MC.

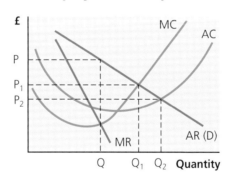

Figure 3.18

In Figure 3.18 the profit-maximising equilibrium is PQ. At this output, **P > MC** and therefore resources are **misallocated**.

The equilibrium where P = MC, P_1Q_1, is **not profit maximising**, although in this diagram profits would still be **excessive**.

Trace the line from Q_2 vertically upwards and see that resources are once again misallocated.

In the heyday of nationalisation when natural monopolies were state controlled, the rule of average cost pricing to remove capitalist profits produced an equilibrium at P_2Q_2 where P < MC.

2.3d Measuring monopoly power

As we move from the theory of a single firm industry to the reality of a firm which controls more than 25% of a specified market, then it becomes clear that there must be degrees of monopoly power. Two methods are commonly used to measure monopoly power.

First, **concentration ratios** measure the proportion of sales going to the four largest firms.

Second, it may be easier to use public records to identify firms that make **large profits** and assume that these profits reflect a degree of monopoly power.

2.4 Monopoly: a point of interest

> A common mistake made by students is to refer to monopolists as having inelastic demand curves.

A monopolist will **never** produce where the demand curve is **inelastic** (Figure 3.19).

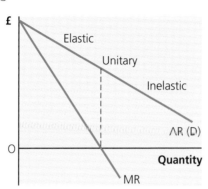

Figure 3.19

The profit-maximising rule is MC = MR. The only place that an equilibrium can be established between MC and MR is where MR is positive. As seen in Figure 3.19, this is where the demand curve is elastic.

2.5 The monopolist and price discrimination

2.5a Two types of discrimination
There are two types of discrimination:
● discrimination between **units sold** to the same buyer, e.g. electricity
● discrimination between **buyers**, e.g. different prices for OAPs

2.5b What turns a single price monopolist into a discriminating price monopolist?
A monopolist cannot price discriminate unless segmentation can clearly **separate** parts of the market and units cannot be **resold** between these parts.

It is easier to separate the market for services than it is to separate the market for goods. Market separation is made possible by:
● time
● transport costs
● national barriers
● quotas and tariffs
● age/sex of the consumer

2.5c Why price discrimination pays, and the perfectly discriminating monopolist
A single price profit-maximising monopolist can make excessive profits but cannot absorb the **consumer surplus**.

Price discrimination pays because it adds some or all of the consumer surplus to the profits.

Only a perfectly discriminating monopolist can absorb all the consumer surplus. In this case, the producer will be able to charge the full price a consumer is

In all other theories of the firm the demand curve is the AR curve, although in perfect competition AR = MR = D.

willing to pay for each unit. Figure 3.20 is interesting because the demand curve is the marginal revenue curve. Profits are still maximised where MC = MR, but the price varies from P_1 to P_N and ABCD is the area of excessive profits.

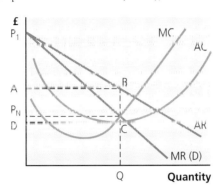

Figure 3.20

2.5d Can discriminatory pricing benefit an economy?

The word 'discrimination' is often associated with bad rather than good, so it is interesting to note that price discrimination can benefit an economy.

First, the output of a perfectly discriminating monopoly will be **higher** than a single price monopolist and the **same** as a perfectly competitive industry.

Second, suppose there is a doctor in the poor part of a country where no single price for treatment will cover costs. The AR and AC curves would not touch, as illustrated in Figure 3.21.

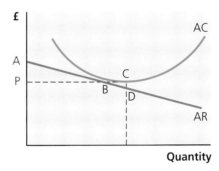

Figure 3.21

However, given price discrimination, as long as the triangle PAB is larger than the triangle BCD, the doctor will remain in business.

3 *The theories of imperfect competition*

3.1 Introduction

Some textbooks take all theories of the firm other than perfect competition as cases of imperfect competition; you can then include monopoly in answer to a question about imperfect competition. Students are often

Given two extreme theories of the firm, namely perfect competition and monopoly, it is reasonable to accept that any industry structure which lies between the two extremes can be included under the collective heading of **imperfect competition**.

In reality some industries comprise many firms, others only a few. However the difference between 'few' and 'many' is defined, it is possible to make a convenient theoretical division between **monopolistic competition** or competition among the many and **oligopoly** or competition among the few.

confused by the use of
the terms 'monopoly'
and 'competition' in
this theory. Remember:
competition results
from many firms and
monopoly is the name
or brand image.

3.2 Monopolistic competition: competition among the many

3.2a Characteristics
- A lot of firms in the industry.
- Free entry into and exit from the industry.
- Products are similar, but differentiated usually by a brand image.
- Product differentiation means that each firm faces a downward-sloping (left to right) demand curve.
- The demand curve is more elastic the **less** differentiated the product and less elastic the **more** differentiated the product.

3.2b The equilibrium of the firm in the short run
This diagram is easy to remember in that you can use the monopoly diagram as your starting position, highlighting the area of excessive profits PABC (Figure 3.22).

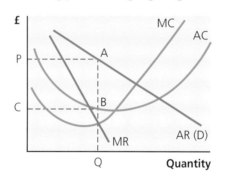

Figure 3.22

In the case of monopoly, barriers to entry maintain this equilibrium, but because there is **free entry** into this industry the excessive profits attract more firms and this shifts each firm's share of demand to the left.

3.2c The equilibrium of the firm in the long run
In the long run each firm will only make **normal profits** (Figure 3.23).

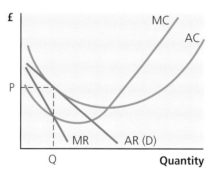

Figure 3.23

As with perfect competition, AR is now tangent to AC but at a point where AC is falling.

In the short run firms can survive making subnormal profits as long as variable costs are covered. However, in the long run firms will leave the industry until only normal profits are made at PQ by those firms left in the industry.

In the short and long run, monopolistic competition produces an equilibrium where there is a **non-optimal allocation** of resources, i.e. where **P > MC**.

Moreover, each firm is **productively inefficient**, i.e. it is not producing at the lowest point on the AC curve. As it produces at a point to the left of where it

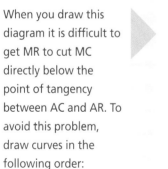

When you draw this
diagram it is difficult to
get MR to cut MC
directly below the
point of tangency
between AC and AR. To
avoid this problem,
draw curves in the
following order:
AC, MC, AR, marking
on P and Q, and finally
draw in MR.

would be productively efficient, a firm is described as producing with **excess capacity**. Only perfectly competitive firms are productively efficient and produce at capacity output in the long run, i.e. the lowest point on the AC curve.

3.3 Oligopoly: competition among the few

3.3a Characteristics

- **Few firms** in the industry where 'few' usually means a number which could manage collusive actions.
- **Capacity output**, which is the lowest point on the AC curve, will occur when a significant proportion of the total market is satisfied. A simple analysis might suggest that if this point is reached when 25% of the market is satisfied, there will be four firms in the industry. At 50% there would be a two-firm industry, or **duopoly**, and so on.
- Other barriers to entry might include **large set up costs, a large advertising budget** and **a proliferation of brands** controlled by one firm.
- A **kinked demand curve** for the firm is likely to exist even though the demand curve for the industry is normal (Figure 3.24). The kink is at the prevailing market price. Raise the price and the firm will lose a lot of customers to competitors. Lower the price and other firms will lower prices rather than risk losing a lot of customers. All the firm will gain is a share of the overall increase in market demand.

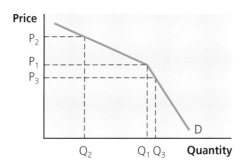

Figure 3.24

- **Administered prices** are an assumption of most theories of oligopoly behaviour. Prices are controlled by the producer rather than determined by the consumer.

> A covert collusion to fix prices is against the law and the cartels in banking and petroleum to fix prices during the 1960s would now be outlawed.

3.3b What determines oligopoly price?

The kinked demand curve suggests that firms have incentives to **collude** in the way that they establish prices and then try to increase market share through **non-price competition**.

If oligopolists agree to restrict output and raise the price, they can make more profits, whereas if they compete, they will be forced towards a normal profit-making situation.

Game theory is often used to explain this dilemma facing oligopolists.

		Firm X	
		Comply	Cheat
Firm Y	Comply	**A**	**B**
	Cheat	**C**	**D**

A If both firms comply with a policy to restrict output and raise prices, they will make excessive profits.

B If Firm Y complies with the agreement but Firm X cheats and expands output, Firm X can make even higher profits than in A, but Firm Y will make a loss.

C If Firm X complies and Firm Y cheats, Y makes profits and X makes a loss.

D If both firms cheat on each other, normal profits will prevail.

The conclusion of this game is that in order to avoid making a loss, both firms will **cheat** and the outcome will be normal profits — the same as if they **competed** with each other.

3.3c Oligopoly and the theory of contestable markets

Contestable markets evaluate the costs of **entering** markets and distinguish between **recoverable** and **sunk** costs. A **perfectly contestable** market will have no sunk costs, while the lower the sunk costs the more contestable the market.

The theory implies that even in industries that contain only a few firms, as long as **actual entry** can take place or **potential entry** is anticipated, then firms will produce at levels which achieve normal profits.

Contestable market theory and **game theory** both suggest that any form of competition will produce competitive rather than excessive profits.

This is interesting because it implies that even in the smallest oligopoly situation, i.e. a duopoly, the firms will be forced into a competitive equilibrium.

The theory was developed by three American professors: Baumol, Panzer and Willig.

4 *Monopoly vs competition*

4.1 The debate

Whether monopoly is bad and perfect competition good is not an economic issue. Whether monopolies are less efficient or more efficient, whether prices are higher or lower under monopoly, are economic issues which have been used to support arguments for and against monopoly and perfect competition.

In reality this debate does not concern itself with the extremes, but rather with the structures that tend towards either monopoly or competition.

4.2 In favour of competition

- Perfect competition produces allocative efficiency **(P = MC)**, productive efficiency **(MC = AC)** and a Pareto-optimum allocation of resources.
- Competition produces greater variety of products.
- Consumer sovereignty involves greater freedom of choice.
- Monopoly produces allocative inefficiency **(P > MC)**, productive inefficiency and is not Pareto efficient.
- In the long run, profits are normal under perfect competition, but can be excessive under monopoly.
- Producer sovereignty exists under monopoly.
- An industry comprising perfectly competitive firms produces a higher output at a lower price P_1Q_1 whereas monopoly produces a lower output at a higher price P_2Q_2 (Figure 3.25).

It is useful to learn this diagram as a simple illustration of why perfect competition is favoured.

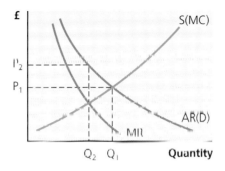

Figure 3.25

4.3 In favour of monopoly

4.3a Removing the given cost assumption

The last argument used in favour of competition assumes that a perfectly competitive industry transformed into a monopoly will inherit the given costs.

In reality the motivation to become a bigger firm in the industry is **economies of scale**. This means it is unreasonable to assume given costs and it is possible for a monopoly to have **lower prices and higher output** than the corresponding perfectly competitive industry. In Figure 3.26, P_1Q_1 represents the competitive equilibrium while P_2Q_2 could be the monopoly equilibrium.

The diagram requires the costs to be reduced sufficiently to shift the intersection of MR and MC to the right of Q_1. At this point the firm would still be making excessive profits.

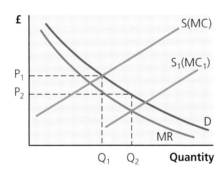

Figure 3.26

4.3b Dynamic efficiency

A third type of efficiency can be introduced into this argument. It is how costs behave **over time**. Firms making large profits are more likely to complete research and development programmes and be more innovative than competitive firms. Their costs will therefore fall much more rapidly over time. Even though these firms remain productively and allocatively inefficient at **one point in time**, they are more dynamically efficient over time.

4.3c Is consumer choice increased under monopoly?

When the British Broadcasting Corporation (BBC) monopolised the airwaves it was argued that it offered a variety of programmes catering for mainstream and minority interests.

More competition over the airwaves produced many more radio stations, but all of them offered a similar diet of popular music interspersed with news items.

4.3d Policy-makers take note

UK policies, particularly those associated with **monopolies and mergers**, are usually framed on the assumption that a monopoly damages the economy.

Although this may be the case, it should not be assumed, as the arguments above bring into question the foundation of the case against monopoly.

5 Contestable markets

5.1 Introduction

The traditional theories of the firm state that as industries are comprised of fewer and fewer firms, so they become less and less competitive until the extreme of monopoly is reached and no competition is assumed. This analysis has been questioned by a number of economists, who suggest that it is still possible for monopoly markets to be contestable if potential firms can enter the industry. There are two main characteristics of a contestable market.

5.2 Characteristics

5.2a Absence of barriers to entry and exit

As long as there are no barriers to entry or exit, markets can be considered contestable. In this situation, the potential to compete rather than actual competition is the prerequisite of contestability.

5.2b No sunk costs

These may or may not be fixed costs. They are non-recoverable costs that firms incur when they enter a market. Fixed costs that are not sunk costs are those that can be partially or totally recovered, i.e. a machine with second-hand value. Perfect contestability requires that there be no sunk costs.

5.3 Implications for government policy

In the past, government policy was triggered by a market share/concentration ratio and therefore, in the UK, a firm with more than a 25% share of a market could be investigated, irrespective of whether the market was contestable or not. The theory of contestable markets suggests that investigations should only take place when markets lack contestability and therefore it may be judged that certain oligopolies and even monopolies are sufficiently contestable not to require investigations for exploitable behaviour.

6 Specialist markets

6.1 Introduction

Across the examining boards there is an expectation that students will familiarise themselves with actual markets and be able to apply the basic economic theory of markets and market failure, which were studied at AS, as well as the theories of the firm and labour markets studied in A2.

6.2 The housing market

This market may be dealt with as one market or segmented into:
- owner occupier
- private rented

- housing associations
- local authority

You will be expected to analyse this market in terms of how supply and demand:
- determine a price
- explain regional price differences
- explain relative prices in the segments identified above
- explain price changes over time
- produce different results with different price elasticities of supply and demand

It is also necessary to consider how the housing market is related to:
- market failure
- government failure
- government policies with particular reference to interest rates
- income elasticity of demand
- environmental problems

6.3 The market for work and leisure

6.3a The opportunity cost

There is an opportunity cost of increasing the amount of time applied to leisure, namely the earnings lost from working. In the opposite direction time spent working imposes a cost of lost leisure. Contracts of employment limit the freedom of the individual to make a free choice between work and leisure and many city workers find themselves forced into working longer hours than they would otherwise choose at the cost of lost leisure time.

6.3b Trends in employment and earnings

The change in real earnings is earnings adjusted for inflation, and this has grown on average by a few per cent per year over recent years.

In 1970 the percentage of people unemployed was relatively low at 2%, rising to above 10% in the mid-1980s, before falling back to just above 3% in 2006.

There are two main measures of unemployment:
- the claimant count, which includes all those people who are registered unemployed
- the ILO unemployment rate, which is based upon a labour force survey and is therefore a sample measure of the percentage of the workforce who are unemployed, but available for work

Over recent years the structure of employment has seen a shift out of manufacturing into the service sector. It is surprising to note that only around 13% of the workforce is in the manufacturing sector.

6.3c Labour costs and labour productivity

- Unit labour costs are all the costs associated with labour divided by output per worker.
- Labour productivity is total output divided by the total labour force.

This is in no way an illustration of how hard labour works, rather a measure of how much capital is employed.

For comparison the statistics can be misleading as a labour-intensive industry will have relatively low labour productivity, whereas a capital-intensive industry will have much higher output per head.

6.3d The sport and leisure market

This market covers:

- holidays
- travel
- the film industry
- television
- theatre
- the music industry
- other forms of entertainment

You will be expected to analyse this market and its segments in terms of:

- how supply and demand determine the price of entering sport and leisure events
- a description of how different market structures can be applied, i.e. a degree of monopoly power for unique events such as the FA Cup Final
- applying income, cross and price elasticity of demand
- how changes in the exchange rate may affect holidays, travel and other exports and imports in this sector
- efficiency, contestability regulation and ownership in these markets
- how the backward-bending supply of effort curves illustrates the relationship between work and leisure

6.3e The labour market

The theory of a labour market is explained in Section D, and how transfer earning and economic rent can be applied to the labour market.

In addition to this it can be seen how labour markets fail to be efficient because of:

- the monopsony power of employers
- the union power of employees
- imperfect information
- lack of mobility
- unemployment
- various types of discrimination

As a result, governments become involved in trying to make labour markets more flexible, often conflicting with trade union goals. This may involve actions on:

- the tax and benefit system
- the minimum wage
- EU directives
- migration policies

In many cases, governments may be trying to deal with the problems of pensions, inequality and poverty.

But governments do not always get it right and may fail to achieve their goals.

6.4 The market for transport

6.4a Introduction

Transport economics involves understanding the way in which people and products are moved around the globe for business and personal reasons. It is analysed from the point of view of the:

- infrastructure, which allows this movement to take place
- vehicles, which carry the passengers and freight

Transport is almost entirely a derived demand in that people and business demand it to move from one place to another. However, there is an element of final demand when people travel for the pleasure of travelling, or are train spotters, or are competitors who race vehicles across land, sea and air.

The main modes of transport are:
- road
- rail
- inland waterways
- sea
- air
- pipelines

6.4b The main issues in transport

These are:
- integrating the various modes of transport into an efficient system
- the degree to which transport should be provided by the private or the public sector
- the sustainability of the resources allocated to transport
- the private and social costs and benefits of transport and productive and allocative efficiency in each mode
- traffic congestions on roads, rail, airspace and airports

6.4c Solving the problems

Mainly because of the externalities involved in the various modes of transport, it is necessary not to view pricing and investment as purely private decisions.

Arguably for roads there is a net economic cost of running the network in terms of pollution and congestion while there is a net economic benefit of running a rail network in terms of less pollution and less congestion on the roads. Does this mean that taxes should be raised on the road network and the vehicles that use it to reflect these external costs, while subsidies should be given to the rail network and trains to reflect their external benefits to society?

Road pricing has become a hot topic of discussion. Should roads become private goods with firms allowed to build them and charge tolls for their use? Should drivers be charged when they use roads or should they pay higher prices for their petrol? Does the London congestion charge allocate resources more efficiently or does it redistribute the problem to other areas of London, producing benefits for one part of London at the expense of another area?

The difficulties involved in measuring total costs and benefits require investment in the transport sector to undergo a cost–benefit analysis. The difficulties faced by cost–benefit analysis include:
- valuing external costs and benefits
- deciding which costs and benefits to include and exclude
- estimating over time the full value of the project

Much of the transport network has been returned to the private sector and subjected to more competition through:

- denationalisation
- deregulation
- franchising

The question then is have these markets and market segments become more competitive or at least more contestable?

6.4d The environment, sustainability and carbon footprints

Transport, in terms of both its infrastructure and the vehicles used, has a damaging effect on the environment and uses up a considerable amount of non-renewable resources. Vehicle manufacturers are looking for ways to produce cars that use sustainable fuels as governments are looking for ways to reduce the carbon footprint caused by transportation.

The carbon footprint is a measure of the impact on the environment of human activities in terms of greenhouse gases. It is measured in units of carbon dioxide.

In order to reduce the carbon footprint, it has been suggested that:

- non-essential travel should be reduced
- public transport should be used wherever possible
- people should adopt car-share schemes
- wherever possible, local products should be consumed
- sustainable fuels should be promoted for travel
- carbon offsets such as tree planting should be used as well as retiring certified carbon credits rather than trading them on to other companies

D The pricing of productive factors

1 Introducing the factors

The economist is not directly concerned with the question of whether the national income is shared out equally or fairly among its recipients, but rather with the forces which determine the size of the shares received by the factors.

All incomes except **transfer payments**, such as state pensions and unemployment pay, are the earnings of the factors of production.

> Transfer payments are income paid out for which no good or service is provided. They should not be confused with transfer earnings.

At its simplest level the rewards to productive factors can be considered as prices:
- the price of labour is a **wage**
- the price of capital is **interest**
- the price of enterprise is **profits**
- the price of land is **rent**

Like other prices, these can be determined in a free market by the interaction of **supply** and **demand**. In markets other than free markets these may be distorted or replaced by other mechanisms.

2 The price of labour

2.1 The form of payment and the factors which influence its size

A salary is a wage paid to workers of a certain status, usually over intervals longer than a week. It is not generally related to a specific number of hours worked.

Payment of a wage is normally made under a legal contract for the services provided by labour.

> Remind yourself of how nominal wages can go up while real wages fall.

It is important to make a distinction between **real** and **nominal** wages. Nominal wages are the units of currency paid to labour. Real wages are the products that can be purchased with any given wage.

The common-sense explanation of the observed large differences in wages between occupations is that labour is **not homogeneous**. There are many differences in skills and abilities and the demand for different workers. These give rise to many labour markets, each with its own supply and demand conditions.

> Wage differentials may exist in money terms but not exist when one takes account of non-pecuniary benefits such as job satisfaction.

Over very long periods of time it is likely that there will be some erosion of wage differentials, but they will never be eliminated because of:
- permanent differences in skills and abilities
- geographical immobility
- **pecuniary** and **non-pecuniary** rewards
- qualification barriers

- unequal opportunity
- imbalances of power between groups of people
- government policies
- dynamic changes and the need for market signals

2.2 The demand for labour

2.2a Basic propositions

Labour is not demanded for itself but for what it can produce: **derived demand**.

The **elasticity** of demand for labour is determined by the elasticity of demand for the product.

The smaller the proportion of total costs accounted for by labour the more **inelastic** is the demand curve.

The more capital can be substituted for labour the more **elastic** is the demand curve.

> Texts often refer to the marginal revenue productivity theory of wages. In fact, it is not a theory of wages but a theory of the demand for labour.

2.2b Marginal revenue productivity

In section B2.1, the marginal and average physical products were given a normal shape. Although physical product is important, it is not the ultimate determinant of labour demand. A firm can be productively efficient, but if it cannot sell its product it cannot make a profit.

What is important is the revenue derived from the sale of the product.

Given the following simplified assumptions:
- profit-maximising entrepreneurs
- one variable factor
- perfectly elastic demand for the product, therefore MPP × price = MRP
- perfectly elastic supply of the productive factor

then the demand curve for labour is MRP below ARP, as illustrated in Figure 3.27.

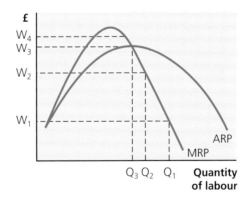

Figure 3.27

At W_1 the entrepreneur will maximise returns by employing Q_1 units of labour. As the wage rate rises up to W_3, less labour will be demanded to maintain maximum profits. At any wage rate above W_3, as illustrated by W_4, it will not be profitable to employ any units of labour and therefore **the demand curve for labour is MRP below ARP**.

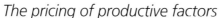

2.2c Shifts in the demand curve for labour

Shifts in the demand curve for labour result from more or less labour being demanded at the same wage rate. This can occur for two main reasons:

- a change in the **physical productivity of labour**
- a change in the **demand for the product**

2.3 The supply of labour

2.3a The individual supply of effort

It is usual to identify the relationship between wages and hours worked by the individual, as illustrated in Figure 3.28.

> Students often confuse the supply of effort, which is how many hours a person will want to work at a given wage rate, with the supply of labour to a given occupation, which is the number of people willing to work at a given wage.

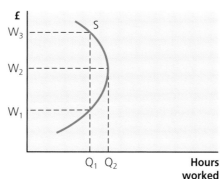

Figure 3.28

Up to W_2, a higher wage will encourage the person to work more hours and have less leisure. After this point a rise in wages will reduce the hours worked as leisure time is of greater value.

An alternative analysis uses indifference curves (Figure 3.29).

> I_1 and I_2 can look as though they will cross as they represent two different situations.

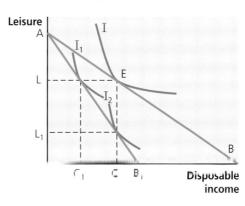

Figure 3.29

A = all leisure

B = all work

E = the chosen balance between leisure (L) and work (C) identified by an indifference curve which is tangent to the line AB

Suppose income tax rises. The highest level of disposable income falls from B to B_1.

If the person wishes to maintain income, she will position herself on AB_1 at L_1C. If she wishes to maintain leisure, she will settle at LC_1.

The debate about whether an average person would choose to sustain leisure or consumption is unresolved.

2.3b The supply of labour to a given occupation

The supply curve for labour in a given labour market is a normal upward-sloping curve from left to right. The higher the wage rate, the more labour is prepared to offer itself for work (Figure 3.30).

Figure 3.30

2.3c Shifts in the supply curve

The slope of the supply curve will vary from one labour market to another. In general, the labour market for **less-skilled** work will produce a **relatively elastic** supply curve, while the **more-skilled** labour markets will produce a **relatively inelastic** supply curve.

2.3c Shifts in the supply curve

More or less labour supplied to a particular labour market at the same wage rate will result from changes in:
- the geographical mobility of labour
- the occupational mobility of labour
- relative wage rates between labour markets

Over a longer period of time, shifts in the supply curve may result from changes in:
- population size
- the structure of the population
- educational attainments
- expectations

2.4 The theory of wage determination in different market conditions

2.4a In a free market

In a labour market where supply and demand are competitive, the **equilibrium wage** rate is determined by the intersection of the demand and supply curves (Figure 3.31).

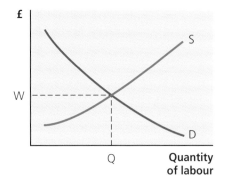

Figure 3.31

2.4b In a market where labour is demanded monopsonistically

If there is a single buyer of labour (monopsony) and competitive selling of labour, then the supply curve becomes separated from the marginal cost curve. This is because as the buyer of labour wishes to attract more labour into the market the wage rate must be raised for all units of labour in order to attract the new labour.

In Figure 3.32, the profit-maximising position is where MC = MRP at WQ. This equilibrium is below the competitive equilibrium at W_1Q_1.

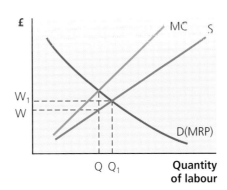

Figure 3.32

2.4c In a market where labour is supplied monopolistically

This is less likely to occur today but, in the past, **trade unions** could gain total control over the supply of labour to a given occupation through a **closed shop** agreement.

In this situation the trade union action could lead to a number of outcomes.

> In order to become an actor it was necessary to be given an Equity Card from the actors' union. There were only a limited number and without one you could not get employment.

- First, the union could raise wages and force the employer to maintain the level of employment by threat of industrial action. Industrial action is a cost to the employer and the company may set aside potential profits to avoid this cost. Therefore the union has forced the wage above the free market equilibrium without any loss of jobs, as illustrated in Figure 3.33.

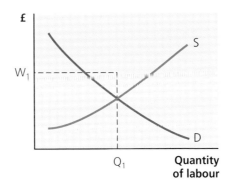

Figure 3.33

- Second, the trade union could raise the wage rate at the expense of lost jobs. In Figure 3.34 union action replaces the supply curve (S) with a curve that is perfectly elastic from the agreed wage rate until it intersects the original supply curve. If the union-controlled wage is W_1, then less labour will be demanded by employers, as illustrated by Q_0, while more people will be attracted to work in this market, with Q_1 seeking employment. The result will be a surplus of workers unable to find a job.

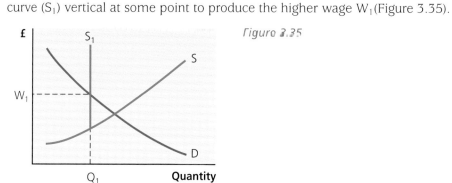

Figure 3.34

The supply curve could change slope or shift to the left as the result of union action.

- Third, the trade union could restrict the supply of labour by such things as qualification barriers or limited apprenticeships. This would make the supply curve (S_1) vertical at some point to produce the higher wage W_1 (Figure 3.35).

Figure 3.35

2.4d In a market where labour is demanded monopsonistically and supplied monopolistically

In the market where labour is demanded monopsonistically, the equilibrium is WQ (Figure 3.36). If a union enters the market, then it has the opportunity to **raise wages and employment** up to W_1Q_1. Past that point, wages can be raised to W_2 and the original level of employment Q can be sustained.

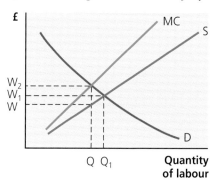

Figure 3.36

This is a source of popular examination questions.

2.5 The theory of wages and wage differentials

Quite often wage differentials are explained using either demand or supply analysis and this can lead to the following misunderstanding: **a high level of demand or an inelastic supply of labour will produce a high wage rate**. This is incorrect in many cases because it is the interaction of supply and demand which determines the wage rate.

This point is clearer if we compare a classically trained violinist with a rock star (Figure 3.37).

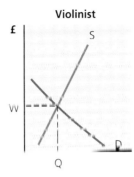
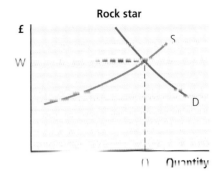

Figure 3.37

This is an Important lesson to remember: good education and a lot of training do not, on their own, ensure a high wage.

The skills required to produce a violinist are likely to give rise to an inelastic supply curve, whereas those required to become a rock star are less and the supply curve is more elastic. However, the demand for the rock star is likely to be higher than the demand for the violinist, resulting in higher wages for the rock star.

It is likely that the demand for refuse collectors exceeds the demand for surgeons, but the limited supply of surgeons produces the higher wage rate (Figure 3.38).

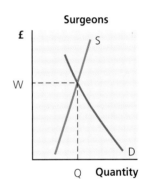

Figure 3.38

Given the interactive analysis above, it is possible to include all the usual points:
- low labour productivity
- qualification barriers
- dangerous jobs
- unique skills
- discrimination by age, sex, race, etc.

There are many social and political reasons used to support a minimum wage.

2.6 A topical issue: the national minimum wage

2.6a In favour

Supporters of a national minimum wage have suggested that it will:
- raise productivity of labour by making it feel more highly valued
- have a shock effect on a company which forces it to reorganise production more efficiently
- raise welfare by redistributing income more evenly

Some economists are concerned that this is interfering with the allocative process of the price mechanism and there are more efficient ways of dealing with poverty, i.e. a reverse income tax.

2.6b Against

Detractors from a national minimum wage highlight the following:
- In order to be effective it will be set at a level above the wage being earned in some labour markets and will cause unemployment Q_1-Q_2 and an involuntary surplus of labour Q_2-Q_3 (Figure 3.39).

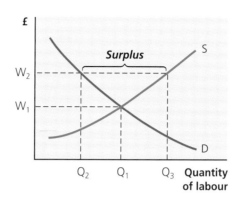

Figure 3.39

W_1 = competitive wage
W_2 = national minimum wage

- There will be pressure to restore wage differentials by those already earning the national minimum wage or just above.
- A black market for labour will develop as there will be people willing to work below the minimum.
- Inflation will erode its real value.

3 The price of capital

3.1 Introduction

By strict definition in economics the price of funds for investment in capital is the **rate of interest**. For example, if an entrepreneur borrows money to build a factory, the price of capital is the rate of interest. If the investment is funded within the firm, the **opportunity cost** of funds is the rate of interest foregone.

As the rate of interest is a price, then under market conditions it will be determined by the forces of demand and supply.

3.2 The demand for investment funds

The demand for investment funds is a major component of the demand for loans.

As with labour, capital is a **derived demand** and changes in either the demand for the product or the revenue productivity of capital will shift the demand for capital.

The demand curve for capital is normally downward sloping from left to right. It is the same as the marginal revenue productivity curve of labour and it is referred to as the **marginal efficiency of investment (capital) curve** (Figure 3.40).

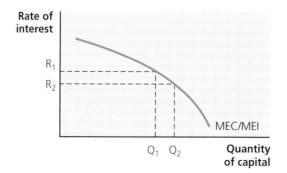

Figure 3.40

The entrepreneur will employ capital up to the point where the rate of interest is equal to the marginal efficiency. If the rate of interest falls from R_1 to R_2, it will be profitable to employ more capital (Q_2 instead of Q_1).

3.3 The supply of investment funds

A society can only provide funds for investment through the process of saving. Saving requires consumption to be less than income as saving is the process of abstaining from consumption, and the rate of interest is the reward for this abstinence.

The richer a society is, the more funds will be available internally for investment.

3.4 The loanable funds theory of interest rate determination

The loanable funds theory suggests that the rate of interest is endogenous to the supply and demand for loanable funds, where the demand for loans to build capital is one component of the total demand which includes mortgage loans, personal loans and other business loans. In Figure 3.41, Q_1 units of capital will be demanded at the equilibrium rate of interest R_1.

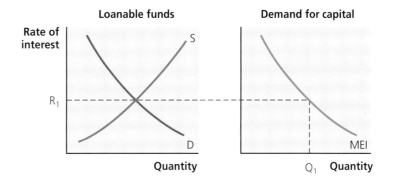

Figure 3.41

4 | The price of enterprise

4.1 Profit

We have so far identified that the entrepreneur pays a single price to employ units of labour and capital.

We have also noted that the return on employing these factors is a downward-sloping MRP or MEI curve (Figure 3.42).

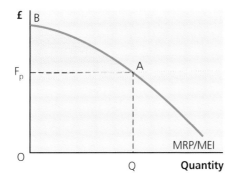

Figure 3.42

This surplus is the
foundation of the
socialist argument
against capitalism.

The rectangle F_pAQO is the total cost of employing the factor and the shaded triangle F_pAB is the **surplus** earnt by the factor, but not paid to the factor. This surplus is the reward to enterprise or profit.

4.2 The role of profit

The uninsurable risk taken by entrepreneurs is rewarded by profits. This risk is very real as many failed entrepreneurs will agree. Only a small proportion of entrepreneurs are successful.

The uncertainties faced by entrepreneurs are all part of the process which allocates and **reallocates** resources. Productive factors are attracted to firms with rising profits and therefore expand the industry, while falling profits and losses cause an industry to contract.

5 The price of land

5.1 From rent to economic rent

The price of land is once again established by the interaction of supply and demand. The term used to describe the price is **rent**.

As all land resources were originally free gifts of nature, any income derived from their ownership was considered to be a **surplus**.

This idea of a surplus reward was applied to all factors of production and the term **economic rent** was used to describe a situation where a productive factor earnt more than the minimum amount required to keep it in its present employment.

5.2 Economic rent and transfer earnings

This should not be
confused with a
transfer payment
which is income, like
unemployment pay,
which is received
without the factor
having to produce
anything.

The minimum income required by a productive factor to keep it in its current employment was termed a **transfer earning**.

In a marketplace for a productive factor such as labour, economic rent (ER) and transfer earning (TE) can be identified (Figure 3.43).

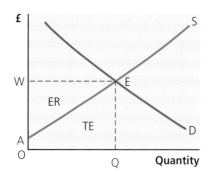

Figure 3.43

The trapezium shape OAEQ shows the minimum income required by labour to remain in this market while the triangle AWE is the surplus.

The slope of the supply curve shows the proportion of economic rent and transfer earnings received by a factor. If it becomes **vertical**, the whole area is economic rent (Figure 3.44).

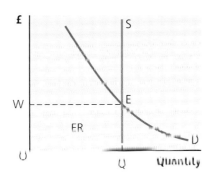

Figure 3.44

If the supply curve is **horizontal**, the whole area is a transfer earning (Figure 3.45).

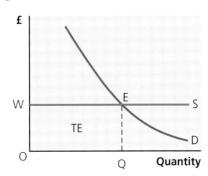

Figure 3.45

In the case of the entrepreneur, **normal profit** is equivalent to a transfer earning while any **excessive profit** is economic rent.

5.3 Economic rent and quasi-rent

Because demand can change quickly while the supply of productive factors adjusts more slowly, there may be a time when productive factors can earn a **temporary** economic rent or quasi-rent.

For example, when the NHS was set up there was a sudden increase in the demand for doctors and dentists as consumers raised consumption to the point where **marginal utility was zero**. As it takes 6 or more years to qualify, there were opportunities for those already qualified to increase their incomes. Gradually over time some of this surplus income was eroded.

Strictly, **economic rent** is permanent and usually refers to unique talents which are difficult to **substitute**.

> How many other, more recent, examples can you think of where labour became short in supply for a period of time?

E A role for government intervention in business activity

1 Introduction

Economists may not agree about whether the level of competition is measured by contestability, concentration ratios, profitability or market share, but they do agree that certain configurations of market structure can shift the balance of power away from the consumer to the producer. In this situation there is an opportunity for the producer to exploit the consumer. For this reason, governments have a policy to promote competition. In the UK a monopoly policy is implemented by the Office of Fair Trading (OFT) and the Competition Commission.

2 Intervention

As well as concentration ratios, the OFT uses market conduct indicators to identify anti-competitive behaviour. These include:

- complaints against a firm
- price distorting activity, such as price discrimination
- merger activity
- changes in return on capital

As it is difficult to define national interest, the 2002 Enterprise Act introduced competition-based tests for business activity that was considered to distort the workings of a free market. The Competition Commission can act upon its decisions by:

- breaking up monopolies
- preventing mergers
- price restraints
- extra tax on profits
- deregulation and removal of entry barriers

3 Ownership

The debate over public or private ownership of industry seems to have been won by the privatisation lobby. The advantages of privatisation are:

- encouraging competition
- promoting enterprise
- increasing efficiency
- a one-off rise in revenue
- reduction in public spending

The disadvantages of privatisation are:
- abuse of monopoly power
- short term gains versus long term investment
- assets sold off too cheaply
- rewarding shareholders rather than serving customers

4 The problem of a natural monopoly

The pricing formula is RPI — X where X is an efficiency gain that is expected to bring about a reduction in real prices.

Many of the previously nationalised industries had the potential when privatised to become natural monopolies, i.e. the most efficient provider in terms of costs was a single firm. To counterbalance this monopoly power, the privatised industry was coupled with a regulatory body: OFTEL for telecommunications, OFGAS for gas, OFGEN for generating electricity and OFWAT for water. These bodies were mainly concerned with controlling pricing to avoid exploitation and the removal of artificial barriers to entry.

5 Economic liberalisation

As well as privatisation, the government has been involved in:
- contracting out services such as refuse collection
- transferring the provision of some services to the market sector from the non-market sector
- creating internal markets, as in the health services
- public–private partnerships (PPPs) to run organisations such as schools and prisons
- the private finance initiative (PFI) to promote public investment
- deregulation to promote free market competition

6 Government failure?

Evaluative comment on government failings is always important at A2.

It is unwise to assume that governments are perfect managers of the market economy, and many examples exist of government failure to get the best out of the resources they have directed. These criticisms have been made regarding resource use in the health and education sectors in particular.

A The national economy

1 The theory of the circular flow of income

1.1 Symbols used in the theory

Y = national income

C = consumption

MPC = marginal propensity to consume, i.e. $\dfrac{\Delta C}{\Delta Y}$

APC = average propensity to consume, i.e. $\dfrac{C}{Y}$

W = withdrawals

    S = savings

    M = imports

    T = taxation

J = injections

    I = investments

    X = exports

    G = government expenditure

AE = aggregate expenditure

K = the multiplier

> Delta (Δ) is used throughout economics to record a change in any variable.

1.2 The basic circular flow model

1.2a The flow of income

Y is a continuous flow which is cut off at specified points in time when national income statistics are measured.

C is a continuous flow in Y. The main additions to this flow are the injections I, X and G. The main subtractions from the flow are the **matching** withdrawals S, M and T.

1.2b The consumption function

Consumption is by far the largest component of aggregate expenditure. An estimate of the relationship between consumption and income is important in macroeconomic management.

Keynesians predict that rising income reduces **MPC** and raises the **marginal propensity to save (MPS)**.

The **Permanent Income Hypothesis** assumes a perception of permanent income which influences actual consumption. Therefore, if a change in income is not perceived as permanent, consumption will not change.

> Popularised by Milton Friedman.

The **Life Cycle Hypothesis** assumes that consumption is planned over a life so as not to pass debts on to future generations.

> Popularised by Franco Modigliani and others.

The last two theories of the consumption function distinguish between a short- and **long-run** effect on consumption of a change in income. There will be less of a reaction in the short run, C_1–C_2, and a greater reaction in the long run, C_1–C_3 (Figure 4.1).

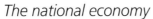

Figure 4.1

When asset values are rising, people feel happy about spending more money, and vice versa.

Changes in the consumption function can result from:
● changes in the distribution of income
● changes in attitude
● changes in access to credit
● the wealth effect

1.2c AD/AS model of equilibrium in the circular flow of income

The aggregate demand curve (AD) comprises the following components: $AD = C + I + G + (X - M)$. The aggregate supply curve represents the total output of the economy at a given point in time and at a given average level of prices. This curve will become vertical at a point where productive capacity is fully utilised, as illustrated in Figure 4.2.

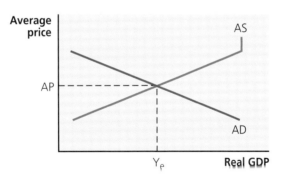

Figure 4.2

An extreme Keynesian diagram assumes that there is no relationship between average prices and changes in output until full employment is reached, as illustrated in Figure 4.3.

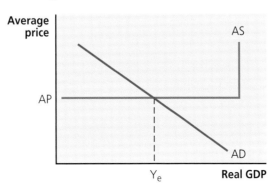

Figure 4.3

An extreme free-market Monetarist assumes that there is no relationship between output and shifts in aggregate demand curves so that the aggregate supply curve is perfectly inelastic, as illustrated in Figure 4.4.

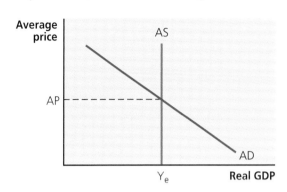

Figure 4.4

Depending upon which diagram is thought to be correct, a shift to the right in the aggregate demand curve will:

- in Figure 4.2, produce inflation and an increase in output
- in Figure 4.3, produce an increase in output up to the point where all resources are fully employed, and then inflation
- in Figure 4.4, produce inflation only

1.2d The withdrawals/injections model of equilibrium in the circular flow of income

A less commonly used diagram, but one that is useful for illustrating a number of issues in macroeconomics, is the model constructed below.

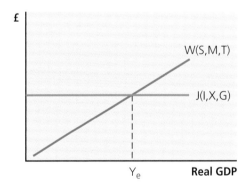

Figure 4.5

In Figure 4.5, real GDP is in equilibrium at Y_e, where the withdrawals from the flow equal the injections into the flow. S, M and T are assumed to be endogenous or induced inside the system, i.e. they change as real GDP changes. I, X and G are assumed to be exogenous or autonomous and are therefore unaffected by changes on the horizontal axis.

1.2e Changes in equilibrium: the multiplier and the accelerator
The multiplier

A change in either the injections into or withdrawals from the circular flow will have a multiple effect on Y. The easiest way to illustrate this is to use the withdrawals injections model. An increase in injections will be illustrated by a shift from $J-J_1$ (Figure 4.6).

> Make sure that you can distinguish carefully between shifts and movements in aggregate demand and aggregate supply curves. Apply the same principles that you used for market supply and demand curves.

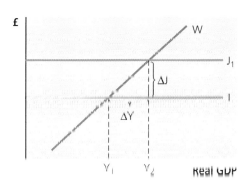

Figure 4.6

The multiplier $K = \dfrac{\Delta Y}{\Delta J}$

The steeper the slope of W, the smaller is the multiplier and vice versa.

The algebraic calculation of this value in a one-sector model is:

$$\frac{1}{MPS} \quad \text{or} \quad \frac{1}{1-MPC} \quad \text{if} \quad \begin{aligned} MPC &= 0.8 \\ MPS &= 0.2 \end{aligned}$$

then $\dfrac{1}{0.2} = 5$

In a two-sector model where government is added, the calculation is:

$$\frac{1}{MPS + MPT} \quad \text{if} \quad \begin{aligned} MPS &= 0.2 \\ MPT &= 0.2 \end{aligned}$$

then $\dfrac{1}{0.2 + 0.2} = \dfrac{1}{0.4} = 2.5$

In a three-sector model where international trade is added, the calculation is:

$$\frac{1}{MPS + MPT + MPM} \quad \text{if} \quad \begin{aligned} MPS &= 0.2 \\ MPT &= 0.2 \\ MPM &= 0.1 \end{aligned}$$

then $\dfrac{1}{0.2 + 0.2 + 0.1} = \dfrac{1}{0.5} = 2$

The obvious assumption is that the injection and withdrawal cancel each other out, but this is not the case. This is because all government expenditure is money spent while only a proportion of the money taxed would have been spent.

It is essential that you grasp the difference between the multiplier and the accelerator.

The same calculation is used whether there is an increase or a decrease in injections or withdrawals.

The interesting point is that an increase or decrease in taxation and government expenditure of the same total produces a **balanced budget multiplier** which always has the value 1.

The accelerator

This is a response to a change in national income. If national income is constant from one year to the next, capital will be replaced at a constant rate. However, if national income is **accelerating**, new capital will have to be purchased.

To illustrate this point, assume there are 1,000 units of capital in the economy of which 100 are replaced each year. Suppose national income doubles. For one year, investment in capital will rise from 100 to 1,100 before setting back at 200 per year or 10%. This acceleration is necessary to maintain the same **capital-output ratio**.

2 Fiscal policy and Keynesian demand management

2.1 Assumptions

Keynesian analysis is based upon the assumption that any economy has a **productive potential** which can only be reached at full employment of resources.

It is also assumed that the economy can settle at **under or over full employment equilibriums** where under is measured by unemployed labour and over by inflation.

To stabilise the economy at full employment, it is necessary to manage aggregate demand.

2.2 Spare capacity and the budget deficit

If the economy is in equilibrium at Y_e in Figure 4.7, government can increase expenditure $J–J_1$ or reduce taxes $W–W_1$ to close the gap.

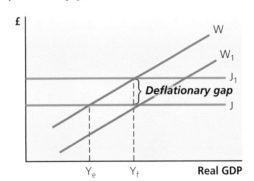

Figure 4.7

2.3 Over capacity and the budget surplus

If the economy is undergoing inflation at full employment, taxes can be raised, $W–W_1$ in Figure 4.8, or expenditure reduced, $J–J_1$, to close the gap.

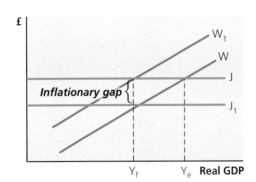

Figure 4.8

3 Monetary policy and the Bank of England

3.1 The functions of the Bank of England

The Bank of England fulfils the following functions:
- government's bank
- bankers' bank
- lender of last resort

- intervenes on the foreign currency market
- supervises other banks with legal power
- manages monetary policy
- seeks to achieve inflation target set by government
- manages note issue

3.2 The structure of the Bank of England

The Bank of England has two totally separate parts:

> Monetarist economists consider this department responsible for much of the inflation suffered in the UK.

The **Issue Department** produces weekly accounts which show the issue of legal tender. It is concerned with the provision of liquidity to the banking system.

The **Banking Department** acts more like a bank in that it accepts loans and makes deposits. Its main customers are the commercial banks and the government.

3.3 The mechanics of monetary policy

3.3a Interest rates

Over recent years the Bank has conducted almost all of its monetary policy through controls over interest rates.

Interest rates have been raised to dampen down excessive demand or reduced if it looks as though the economy is moving into recession.

The **Monetary Policy Committee** meets regularly to determine interest rates, but the gap between decisions and the time lags involved in economic events have led to the criticism that its actions are often 'too little too late' or 'too much too early'.

3.3b Other techniques

In the past, the Bank has used a variety of techniques to pursue its monetary policy. Although it does not currently use any technique other than interest rates, the other options remain available. They include:

- **Open market operations:** selling government debt removes cash from the economy while buying back debt returns it.
- **Funding:** changes the structure of the National Debt by issuing more long-term securities and fewer short-term securities. This reduces liquid assets in the banking system.
- **Quantitative controls:** previous governments have used ceilings to restrict bank lending.
- **Quantitative guidance:** the Bank could encourage banks to lend to exporters, but not lend for domestic consumption.
- **Special deposits:** a cash call from the Bank to a commercial bank — the account is frozen and cannot be included in the bank's liquid reserves.

> These ways are not totally independent as a change in interest rates will affect the money supply and vice versa.

3.4 The targets of monetary policy

The main target of monetary policy is the level of monetary demand. This can be affected in one of two ways:

- by changing interest rates
- by changing the supply of money

There are two broadly opposed views to targeting monetary policy.

Keynesians argue that **fiscal policy** is the important target and monetary policy is not important on its own, but needs to accommodate the expenditure and taxation policy. Therefore, it is not necessary to have monetary targets, and interest rates only need to be adjusted in order to aid the financing of the **public sector borrowing requirement (PSBR)**.

Monetarists base their argument on the **Quantity Theory of Money** which was first popularised by **Irving Fisher**. The equation MV = PT where:

> M = money stock
> V = velocity of circulation
> P = average price level
> T = number of transactions

The modern exponents of monetarism include F. A. Hayek and M. Friedman.

is the foundation of modern monetarism.

Crudely stated, M and V make up **monetary demand** while P and T could be translated into **national income**.

Monetarists argue that it is important that the money supply does not grow out of phase with the growth of productivity/output in the economy. If it does, then **inflation** and **deflation** will damage the economy.

Among the Monetarists there is an interesting debate. One side argues that the money supply must be managed by controls over **cash**. This will determine the money supply through the bank credit multiplier and interest rates can be established through market forces. The other side argues that the more direct and precise method of control is through managed **interest rates**.

3.5 An independent Bank of England

On 6 May 1997, the Bank of England was given its independence and charged with maintaining an **inflation target**.

Advantages
- The profile of monetary policy has been raised and will act as a discipline on government spending.
- From a Monetarist perspective, the Bank is now being asked to manage the only thing it can control, i.e. inflation.
- The Bank will no longer have to follow the Treasury against its better judgement.
- Reconciling the conflict between monetary policy and managing the **National Debt** will be less of a problem. Previously, the PSBR and interest rate targets were often seen as incompatible with monetary and inflation targets.
- The commercial banks expect the Bank to maintain stability in the banking sector.

Disadvantages
- From the government's perspective, borrowing targets may have to be changed.
- The Keynesians will see a weakening of fiscal policy and the pursuit of demand management and difficulties in achieving employment level targets.

● The Bank may overreact on inflation targets and push the economy into recession.

● If cost–push inflation exists, the Bank may be helpless in its pursuit of an inflation target

4 Free-market Monetarists vs Keynesians

At the extreme, these two schools of thought produce opposing views

Monetarists believe that the free market has a tendency to self-regulate through the forces of supply and demand which will cause it to settle at a high (natural) level of employment. The profit motive and private property rights will ensure economic growth. All that government needs to do is maintain the conditions under which the free market can function effectively. The money supply needs to be expanded in line with output and price stability will be maintained. They also believe that many problems like inflation are the result of misguided attempts to manage the economy.

At the other extreme, Keynesians believe the free market has weak self-regulatory powers and is prone to market failures that can cause low employment equilibriums and low economic growth. Left to itself, the market will gradually be dominated by large firms which shift the balance of economic power towards the producer. Powerful unions and unfettered foreign exchange markets can cause cost–push inflation and large cyclical fluctuations in economic activity. To prevent these events, government must fine tune the economy using mainly fiscal policy supplemented by monetary policy.

The differences between these schools of thought are highlighted below:

> Strictly speaking, monetarism is only about the relationship between changes in the supply of money causing changes in nominal national income. However, Monetarists are usually associated with free-market capitalism, so our reference to Monetarists will refer to this broader description.

Monetarists	Keynesians
Importance of money and monetary policy.	Importance of aggregate demand and fiscal policy.
A natural level of unemployment when prices are stable.	Low employment equilibriums which can be managed away.
Unemployment can result from the monetary mismanagements which cause inflation and deflation.	Unemployment is caused by deficient aggregate demand and can be associated with cost–push inflation.
An excessive increase in the money supply will raise nominal national income and probably cause inflation.	A cost–push inflation needs an accommodating increase in money supply if deflation is to be avoided.
One cause of inflation.	Two causes of inflation.
Unemployment can be reduced by monetary stability and adjustments to the supply side of the economy.	Unemployment can be reduced by increasing demand and introducing income policies and import controls.

Aggregate supply and demand curves can be used to illustrate the difference.

Keynesians would argue that the aggregate supply function is perfectly elastic up to full employment and therefore demand management can be used to shift AD_1 to AD_2 (Figure 4.9).

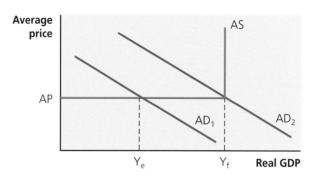

Figure 4.9

Monetarists argue that the aggregate supply function is vertical at the natural level of unemployment. AS can be shifted to the right, AS_1, by supply-side policies and prices will remain stable if monetary demand shifts in line with output $AD–AD_1$ (Figure 4.10).

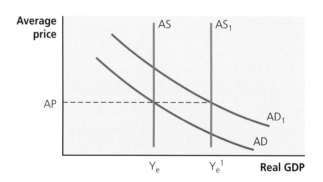

Figure 4.10

5   Replacing demand management with supply-side policies

The aim is to improve the workings of the market, increasing both competition and incentives, thus adding to the supply potential of the economy. There are three main policy groupings:

Market freedom:
- deregulation
- promotion of competition
- curbing monopoly power in labour markets
- privatisation
- removing barriers to the flow of capital
- reinforcing private property rights

Incentives:
- tax reductions
- profit-related pay
- employee share ownership
- wider share ownership
- encouraging start-up business

Cost reductions:
- reductions in national insurance
- improvements in the quality of labour

B International trade

1 The gains from trade

The fundamental point about international trade is that **everyone benefits**. This is easy to see using examples where each country has an **absolute advantage**. It is harder to understand where a country has only a **comparative advantage**.

Absolute advantage exists where, given the same resources, one country can produce more than the other.

Comparative advantage exists when a country has an absolute disadvantage in its production, but it has a lower **opportunity cost** for producing one product. Let us go through an example.

Suppose countries A and B both produce two products — wheat and barley — and, given the same amount of resources, they can produce the following totals:

	Wheat	Barley
A	75,000	100,000
B	50,000	80,000

Country A has an absolute advantage in the production of both wheat and barley.

Should the countries specialise? The answer is 'yes' if their opportunity costs are different.

	Opportunity cost of producing 1 unit of wheat	Opportunity cost of producing 1 unit of barley
A	$^4/_3$ **B**	$^3/_4$ W
B	$^8/_5$ B	$^5/_8$ **W**

The opportunity costs are different, so if each country specialises in the product for which it has a comparative advantage, there will be gains from trade.

Opportunity costs are important because not only do they tell us that A will specialise in wheat and B in barley, but they also provide the **limits to exchange** between which the **terms of trade** must lie for both countries to benefit. The terms of trade must lie between $^5/_8$W and $^6/_8$W for one unit of barley.

In any example of comparative advantage it is always possible to produce more of both products after specialisation. This may require some, but not all, resources to be shifted to the product with the lower opportunity cost.

One final point is that if the opportunity costs are the **same**, then there is no way that resources can be reallocated to produce gains from trade. For example, if there was a very slight change to the previous example:

	Wheat	Barley
A	62,500	100,000
B	50,000	80,000

To work out the opportunity cost of wheat production, given an output, place the barley total **over** the wheat total. Remember that if statistics are given in the form of costs, then the opportunity cost would be found for wheat by placing the barley number **under** the wheat number.

This could be written as 1 unit of wheat must trade for between $^4/_3$ units of barley and $^8/_5$ units of barley.

Country A still has absolute advantage in the production of wheat and barley, but the opportunity costs are now the same (check the calculation yourself). In this situation, there can be **no trade gains**.

2 Measuring the terms of trade

Direct trade of wheat for barley gives rise to the **real terms of trade**. To measure the terms of trade given prices, the following calculation is used:

$$\text{terms of trade} = \frac{\text{index number for the change in export prices}}{\text{index number for the change in import prices}} \times 100$$

Suppose, in year 1, export prices rose by 10% and import prices by 25%. The terms of trade would be:

$$\frac{110}{125} \times 100 = 88$$

The fall in the terms of trade is described as **unfavourable** as more exports would have to be sold to buy the same quantity of imports.

In year 2, suppose the export index rose to 125 while the import index rose to 130:

$$\frac{125}{130} \times 100 = 96.2$$

> Remember that the terms of trade must rise to be described as favourable. It does not have to be above 100 unless a comparison is being made with a base year.

The rise from 88 to 96.2 is a **favourable** movement as less exports will have to be sold to buy the same quantity of imports.

3 Misleading terminology

The terms of trade descriptions, **favourable** and **unfavourable**, can be misleading when one looks at the impact on the balance of payments.

A fall in export prices and a rise in import prices will bring about an **unfavourable fall in the terms of trade**. However, if the demand for both imports and exports is elastic, the lower price for exports will **increase** sales revenue from foreign countries while the higher price for imports will reduce the sales revenue going abroad. This can be described as having a **favourable effect on the balance of payments** as less sterling is being spent on foreign products and more foreign currency is being spent on UK products.

> This apparent confusion is a common source of examination questions.

Alternatively, a **favourable** movement in the terms of trade, under these conditions, will have an **unfavourable** effect on the balance of payments.

4 Free trade or protection

4.1 Introduction

The theory of comparative advantage produces trade gains which have been described as giving benefits to both trading partners in terms of higher

output. Many economists argue that, in theory, the world economy would be most efficient if there was totally free trade and market forces allocated resources.

However, the reality is that the world trading model is a complex interaction of national economies which have created trade barriers against all countries, some countries, all products or some products.

4.2 The main methods of protection

Tariffs raise the price of imports either by a specific amount or by a percentage of the import price.

Quotas limit the imports from a certain country or a particular industry to a specific total per time period.

Domestic policies include a variety of options such as:
- subsidies to domestic industry
- legislation
- differential tax rates
- quality control
- minimum standards
- 'Buy British' campaigns

4.3 The case for protection
- Protection of infant industries.
- Protection of a senile industry while it regenerates.
- To counter unfair trading practices which may include dumping or protection from a foreign monopoly supplier.
- Protection against illegal imports, i.e. drugs.
- Protection of industries for national security reasons.
- To protect employment in industries sensitive to foreign competition.
- A source of revenue for government.

> 'Dumping' means a country sells its products abroad at below cost. This could be to clear an oversupply or it could be an attempt to bring down a domestic industry and penetrate a new market.

4.4 The case against protection
- Protecting an inefficient industry becomes a permanent rather than a temporary misallocation of resources.
- Infant industries never grow up.
- Retaliation from other countries.
- Raises the cost of living.
- Restricts consumer choice.
- Ignores the theory of comparative advantage.

5   *Supranational organisations*

5.1 Customs union

This refers to a group of countries which remove trade barriers between themselves and **erect a common external barrier** against the rest of the world.

This is usually a movement towards freer trade, although technically it could be a move towards protection, depending upon the original position of the countries that join.

Agriculture is an exception that will be looked at on its own.

In the case of the European Union, when it was set up free trade was improved, not only by removing internal tariffs but also by attempting to create a common external tariff at the lowest level.

Advantages
- Trade creation.
- Single large market.
- Industries can expand and take advantage of economies of scale.
- Theory of comparative advantage.
- Over the longer term more competition will have beneficial effects on enterprise and efficiency.

Disadvantages
- Trade-diverting effect.
- Advantages will not be evenly distributed.
- Countries located near the centre of the market will receive more benefits.
- Some industries in some countries will not survive the increased competition.

This is a difficult diagram to understand, but it is an important diagram to be able to draw and explain.

The process of trade creation and diversion when a customs union is established can be illustrated using Figure 4.11:

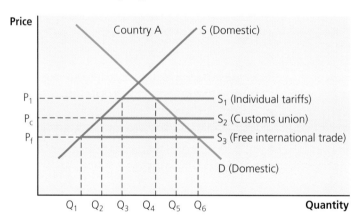

Figure 4.11

P_1 If international trade takes place and all countries have their own individual tariffs in place, the supply curve will become perfectly elastic at P_1.

P_c If a customs union with a lower common external tariff is introduced, trade will be diverted from country A's domestic producers (Q_3-Q_2), net trade creation will occur between Q_4 and Q_5 and imports will be Q_5-Q_2.

P_f If there were free international trade, more domestic production would be diverted to importers (Q_2-Q_1) and there would be further net trade creation (Q_5-Q_6).

A customs union for less developed countries
The arguments for and against a customs union among less developed countries are similar with one important addition. The EU is a powerful union and individual, less developed countries find it difficult to act alone, but as a group of countries they will be able to protect themselves against EU policies that they may see damaging their economies.

5.2 A single European market

This is one stage further on from a customs union. All the rules of the customs union apply and in addition there are other features:

- complete freedom of movement for productive factors
- no customs hold-ups
- common commercial laws
- single European currency
- standardised quality control
- open tender for public contracts

5.3 A free-trade area

This is different from a customs union in that each country maintains its own external barrier against the rest of the world while removing barriers to those countries which are members. An example is the **European Free-Trade Area** (EFTA).

With no common external tariff it is necessary to have a **re-export tariff**. For example, if country A has a 50% tariff on one product while country B has a 10% tariff, then a 40% re-export tariff will be necessary in B to stop products entering the free-trade area and breaching A's tariff.

Other differences are that only goods move freely in a free-trade area and there is no centralised political structure.

5.4 A European Union problem: the CAP

The only industry within the EU that has its own set of rules and does not abide by the rules of a customs union is agriculture.

The Common Agricultural Policy (CAP) has a minimum pricing policy for 90% of its products which distorts the free market.

Advantages

- Unified national controls.
- Stabilised farm incomes.
- Expanded agricultural output.
- Reduced fluctuations in output.
- Created surpluses to be used in bad years.

Disadvantages

- Most prices are above market clearing levels.
- Surpluses are not cleared and are costly to sustain.
- Consumers face higher prices.
- Consumers face less choice.
- Consumers pay higher taxes.
- Non-EU farmers are denied a competitive marketplace through import levies.
- Non-EU countries have products dumped on them through export subsidies.

A simple solution?

Observe the rules of a customs union, support farm incomes, but leave prices alone and let them clear at the free market level.

C The balance of payments

1 Some definitions

Financial news items often concentrate on this account which is somewhat misleading as the **current balance** is much more significant as an indicator of the well-being of the economy.

Balance of payments: the difference between the total payments into and out of a country measured in domestic currency over a given time period.

Balance of payments current account: this is usually referred to as the **current balance** — the difference between the total value of **goods** and **services** exported and imported over a given time period.

Visible balance of trade: the difference between the total value of **goods** exported and imported over a given time period.

Invisible balance: the difference between the total value of **services** exported and imported over a given time period.

Capital account: since the introduction of new accounting rules in 1998, this account only includes details of transactions in fixed and non-financial assets. Its main component is asset transfers by migrants and it is now only a small component of the balance of payments.

Financial account: this includes almost all the components that were originally in the pre-1998 capital account except those items that appear above in the new capital account. It includes all unofficial movements in terms of the sale and purchase of companies and portfolio investment, as well as the official flows mainly from and to the foreign exchange reserves.

Official financing: this is a part of the capital account which offsets the positive or negative currency flow generated by all other parts of the balance of payments.

Net errors and omissions: originally the balance item, this represents an estimate of the sum of errors and omissions in the accounts.

Exports or imports FOB: this means free on board and is a value of tangible goods excluding the cost of insurance and transport.

Exports or imports CIF: this measures the value of goods including a contract for the cost of insurance and freight.

2 Why does the balance of payments always balance?

Because official financing is part of the financial account, it is often said that a current account deficit will equal a financial account surplus and vice versa.

Quite simply, it is an accounting identity. Any negative or positive currency flow which results from the current balance and unofficial financial account and capital account transactions will be offset by official financing. For example, if there is a current account deficit of −£10 million and a deficit on the unofficial capital account of −£15 million, the currency flow is −£25 million and this will be financed officially by running down the foreign exchange reserves by +£25 million.

A positive currency flow will produce an equal and opposite negative official financing figure. In this case, foreign exchange reserves will be increased.

3 Equilibrium and disequilibrium on the current balance

Disequilibrium on the current account can be either a deficit or a surplus, which is persistent. Statistically, every month there is likely to be a temporary disequilibrium as the likelihood of the current balance being zero is small. Therefore equilibrium exists when the surpluses tend to be offset by deficits over a significant time period.

When currencies are **floating** there is an inbuilt corrective mechanism to persistent disequilibrium. The currency will tend to **depreciate** as a deficit reduces the demand for a currency relative to its supply, and **appreciate** with a surplus.

A disequilibrium requires corrective action when a currency is **fixed** against other currencies. The options we will consider are:

> Remember that reference to a floating system means change through appreciation and depreciation, while a fixed system requires a change from one agreed point to another and is termed revaluation or devaluation.

- **devaluation** of the currency
- **revaluation** of the currency
- **reflation** of domestic demand
- **deflation** of domestic demand

The choice of policy will depend upon whether the economy is at:
- full employment
- under full employment
- over full employment

and it will be assumed that the sum of demand elasticities for imports and exports is greater than one. The reason for this is explained by the Marshall-Lerner Condition (see section 5).

A persistent surplus at under full employment: this will require a **reflation** of domestic demand which will increase output and employment, increase the demand for imports and redirect some potential exports into the home market.

A persistent surplus at over full employment: this will require a **revaluation** of the currency which will relieve the pressure of demand on domestic products through lower import prices and higher export prices.

> Knowing the correct changes is not so easy in practice.

A persistent surplus at full employment: this will require a little **revaluation** to correct the current account imbalance and a little **reflation** to maintain full employment.

A persistent deficit at under full employment: this will require a **devaluation** to reduce the price of exports, raise the price of imports and boost demand for domestic products.

A persistent deficit at over full employment: this will require a **deflation** of demand to control inflation, reduce demand for imports and switch some unsold domestic products into export markets.

A persistent deficit at full employment: this will require a little **devaluation** to correct the current account imbalance and a little **deflation** to maintain full employment.

Finally, it should be noted that small imbalances can be dealt with by microeconomic policies which may involve adjustments to taxes or tariffs among other things.

4 Can a country run a persistent disequilibrium on the current balance?

Countries like the UK and USA have run deficits on the current account for long periods of time while countries like Japan have run surpluses for similar periods. Can this continue indefinitely? Although reality may contradict this, the theoretical answer is 'no'.

A **persistent deficit** would require a country to have unlimited gold and foreign exchange reserves or an ability to borrow foreign currency indefinitely from the rest of the world. Given a fixed rate, speculators are able to force a currency devaluation, as occurred in the UK in 1967 and 1992. When currencies are floating, depreciation seems to allow the deficit to continue for a longer period.

A **persistent surplus** is less of a problem for the country concerned but, by definition, other parts of the world must be in deficit and it is likely that these countries will apply pressure on the surplus country to revalue, reflate or allow an upward float. Japan has certainly felt such pressure, particularly from the USA.

5 Disequilibrium and the Marshall-Lerner Condition

'One' is often written as 'unity' in economics, so do not be confused.

The **Marshall-Lerner Condition** states that for a devaluation to be successful, the sum of the demand elasticities for imports and exports must be **greater than one**. If the sum is equal to one, a change in the rate of exchange will leave the balance unchanged in percentage terms; if the sum is less than one, a devaluation will worsen the balance.

In percentage terms the change will be the same; in real terms it will differ if the value of imports and exports differ to begin with:

(1) 100 − 100 = 0
A 10% change in both and
110 − 110 = 0.

(2) 200 − 100 = 100
A 10% change in both and
220 − 110 = 110.

The example below illustrates how a devaluation of the pound in the UK will have no effect on the current balance in percentage terms.

A devaluation of 3%

Price elasticity	Price change	Change in demand	Change in revenue
0.25	**Exports** Domestic output prices unchanged in sterling, 3% depreciated in foreign currency	+ 0.75%	+ 0.75%
0.75	**Imports** Import prices rise by 3% in terms of sterling	− 2.25%	+ 0.75%

The result of the above is that the change in sterling revenue received from exports and the change in sterling expenditure on imports rise by the same amount. The balance therefore remains unchanged.

If this example is repeated for a price elasticity sum which is less than one, the balance worsens. It only improves if the sum is greater than one.

D Foreign exchange

1 PPP: the earliest theory of exchange rates

Purchasing power parity (PPP) between exchange rates is said to exist when equivalent amounts of the currencies have identical purchasing power in their respective countries.

It is a fact that exchange rates do not equalise purchasing power. Supporters of the theory say this is because there is not a free market and the rate cannot settle where purchasing power is equalised.

The most powerful argument against PPP as a theory of exchange rate determination is that the supply and demand for currency is only determined by those current and capital account items that are traded across international boundaries. Those products which are not traded internationally and have different prices will still be included in any measure of PPP.

2 Simple exchange rate theory

> Students are often confused by the fact that it is demand that causes both the supply and demand for a currency, i.e. the demand for imports and the demand for exports.

The demand for a currency is determined by the **demand** for exports.

The supply of a currency is determined by the **demand** for imports.

The price of a currency in a free market is determined by the interaction of supply and demand, as illustrated in Figure 4.12.

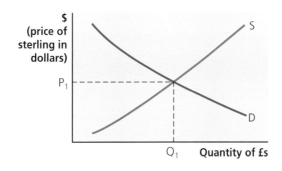

Figure 4.12
Price of sterling

P_1Q_1 is the market clearing equilibrium. It is important to note that you can only measure the price of **one currency** in units of **another currency**. In this case sterling is measured in dollars.

The elasticity complication: in fact in Figure 4.12 the supply curve is drawn on the assumption that the demand for imports is elastic — this means that as the price of imports falls, more currency is supplied to buy more imports.

> Refer back to Unit 1 (B, 4.4) which looks at the relationship between revenue and elasticity.

However, the same amount of currency would be provided to buy more imports if demand is **unitary**, and less currency would be supplied to buy more imports if demand is **inelastic**.

Although the demand for currency is **always** downward sloping from left to right, the supply curve could be as illustrated in Figure 4.13.

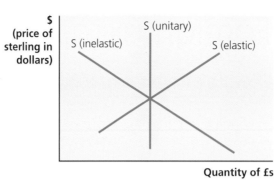

Figure 4.13
Supply of sterling
given different demand
elasticities for imports

Changes in the equilibrium rate of exchange will result from **shifts** in either the supply or demand curve for a currency. Common causes are:

- change in world prices
- development of an import substituting industry
- differential rates of inflation
- changes in interest rates
- other changes in capital flows not caused by interest rates
- economic growth
- government policies

3 Fixed or floating rates of exchange

3.1 The case for floating rates

The free market does it best. One argument suggests that in a dynamic world economy, exchange rates have to change and, left to market forces, these will occur as required.

Fluctuating exchange rates have often been criticised for disturbing and distorting economies. Some economists, however, say that these fluctuations are just a symptom of deeper-seated economic problems, and therefore the floating exchange rate is not the cause.

> Speculation under a fixed-rates system is sometimes referred to as a speculator's 'paradise', i.e. a no-lose situation.

Floating rates reduce the chance of a currency becoming significantly over- or under-valued. This means that the massive speculations associated with fixed rates cannot occur.

3.2 The case for fixed rates

If floating rates cause instability, then fixed rates create the **stability** that traders require. A businessman agreeing to buy a foreign product for future delivery will be guaranteed the sterling price under a fixed-rate system.

Monetarist economists have argued that a fixed exchange rate imposes a monetary discipline upon governments which might otherwise be inclined to fiscal excess.

3.3 The difference between fixed and floating currencies

Both fixed and floating currencies have their prices determined by **market forces**. The only difference between them is that a **free float** involves no intervention

by government. A fixed system is only fixed in the sense that government says overtly that it will intervene in the markets and buy or sell currency to maintain a target or par value for that currency. Some market movement will be allowed either side of par before intervention takes place.

In fact, in most countries with floating currencies it is not a free float, but a **managed float**. Here governments intervene **covertly** as they have no set target for a par value, but they do have a preferred rate.

> Often a government will intervene if the exchange value moves close to what it considers to be an undesirable rate.

4 The practice of foreign exchange

4.1 A brief history

A **gold standard** existed during the nineteenth century and any net deficits or surpluses on trade were settled with a transfer of gold between countries. This had an automatic **reflationary or deflationary** effect on domestic demand and brought about a correction to the balance of payments.

The gold standard was abandoned during the First World War and only partially resurrected after a meeting at Bretton Woods in 1944 when the **Gold Exchange Standard** was used as the basis for fixed rates of exchange. The central bank of each country could settle debts in either gold or dollars which were transferable into gold at an official level. **Devaluations** and **revaluations** were also acceptable ways of adjusting the value of a currency that became over- or under-valued.

During the 1970s, monetary mismanagement and an ever-increasing gap between the market price and official price of gold led to most countries adopting a floating system for their exchange rates. Europe tried to maintain some degree of control over currency exchange which ultimately led to the events of 1999 and the **single European currency**.

4.2 The single European currency

There is still a significant question mark about whether the UK should join a system that will fix the value of sterling irrevocably to the **euro** and the euro will be expected gradually to replace sterling in all transactions.

In favour

> Many economists consider this to be a considerable political overestimate.

A report from the EU commission stated that the **efficiency gain** from removing currency uncertainty and exchange rate costs may be worth as much as 10% of GNP.

There will be **cost advantages** as changing currencies is time-consuming and costly.

A single currency will remove an artificial restriction to free trade within Europe and bring about a more **efficient allocation of resources**.

The euro will create more **price stability** in individual countries by removing any opportunity to speculate on price movements in their currency.

Traders in Europe will be **certain of the price** they agree under contract for future delivery.

Analysis of monetary and price stability throughout Europe since 1945 shows the UK lagging behind the other main countries, particularly Germany. It may therefore be an advantage to join a system whose members have a **better track record**.

The **monetary discipline** imposed upon the UK government will act as a discipline on fiscal policy, particularly in the run-up to a new election.

Against

Some economists estimate the cost advantages of joining as less than 0.1% of GNP which has to be measured against considerable **private and external costs** involved in the transition to a single currency.

Price stability is not guaranteed under the European Central Bank. It will be run by a cartel, and history has shown that when decisions are made by a group of people with different political agendas and target numbers, it is likely they will agree on the **larger number**.

As each economy is likely to grow at a different rate, there is more support for flexibility in exchange rate and interest rate policy outside the single currency. Arguably, any adjustments to these variables can solve certain problems by affecting everyone a little rather than a few people a lot if **unemployment** results.

The UK will no longer be able to use its Keynesian fiscal policy to manage the overall level of economic activity.

An often forgotten problem is the rate at which sterling is irrevocably fixed to the euro. As long as there are interest rate differentials, it is likely that the currency value is distorted, and once a decision is made there is no going back.

4.3 The foreign exchange market (FOREX)

The FOREX provides traders, tourists and investors with the facility to **exchange currencies**. Because there are a large number of operators in the market, uniform products and quick responses to price differences, the FOREX is often used as an example of a **near perfect market**.

The FOREX is subdivided into three main markets:
- spot
- forwards
- futures

The spot market is for current deals which are made at today's price for delivery today.

Forward deals offer traders certainty in an uncertain market in as much as they can agree today a price for currency delivered in the future.

Futures are contracts where an **option** to buy currency in the future is purchased. If the option is not exercised by a certain date, it becomes void.

These became important after June 1972 when the UK moved from a fixed to a floating rate.

Speculators rather than traders tend to use options.

4.4 The eurocurrency market

This market is quite distinct from the FOREX. It is not a market for buying and selling currencies but a market for accepting deposits and making loans in foreign currency.

Bank deposits are made in a currency other than the national currency by a non-resident of the country.

The market developed to circumnavigate national regulations. It only accepts large deposits and it makes loans on flexible terms with few formalities.

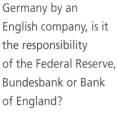

For example, if dollars were deposited in Germany by an English company, is it the responsibility of the Federal Reserve, Bundesbank or Bank of England?

It is now a very large market and an important source of loans for capital projects. As there is no central authority controlling its activities, there is uncertainty surrounding the division of responsibility in the case of heavy losses. Does the responsibility rest with the country where the deposit was made, the country where the company making the deposit is owned, or the country whose currency is being used?

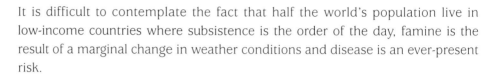

E The less developed world

1 A real difference

It is difficult to contemplate the fact that half the world's population live in low-income countries where subsistence is the order of the day, famine is the result of a marginal change in weather conditions and disease is an ever-present risk.

These generalisations need to be tempered by the thought that there are many rich people in poor countries and many poor people in rich countries.

2 The characteristics of less developed countries (LDCs)

- high population growth
- higher birth and death rates
- lower average age
- higher levels of illiteracy
- few middle income earners
- high concentration of workers employed in agriculture and extractive industries
- low skill levels
- subsistence incomes
- undeveloped social infrastructure
- few public and merit goods
- immature financial structure
- unsound currency

3 Causes

3.1 Population growth

Fast population growth is often the antithesis of economic growth which, by definition, is of a per capita nature.

> A rational explanation of large families is that in the absence of pensions and welfare benefits and with high child mortality, many children are good security in old age and infirmity.

Unfortunately, inhabitants of LDCs can be portrayed as uneducated people incapable of determining what is in their best interest. Sterilisation and restriction of family size need to be imposed, so the argument goes.

3.2 Lack of natural resources

Oil made the Middle East rich. However, natural resources do not always ensure high incomes in the same way that the lack of natural resources does not always ensure low incomes, although it is often a contributing factor.

3.3 Lack of physical capital

It is a **necessary** though not **sufficient** condition of high-income countries that

they have high capital–labour ratios. LDCs have much less physical capital per head of population.

3.4 Immature financial structure

To facilitate the growth of physical capital it is necessary to have a sophisticated financial system which can bring together **savers** and **investors**.

3.5 Social capital

An infrastructure of transportation and communication networks is necessary for the development of trade.

3.6 Human capital

Without the resources to devote to education and health, the workforce in LDCs is less productive in similar jobs and less able to do more productive jobs.

3.7 Culture and tradition

Officially this does not exist, but in reality there is still much evidence of labour immobility.

Arguably many LDCs have been held back by various institutional factors. The caste system in India did not allow labour mobility that would bring about an efficient distribution of labour skills. Many religions do not embrace the ideals of capitalism, economic growth and secular prosperity. Societies which do not encourage **equal rights for women** will also languish down the economic league table.

4 *Solutions*

4.1 Is it economic growth or economic development?

Economic growth is an increase in productive capacity per capita, while economic development has a wider remit and can take place without there being any economic growth.

Development can occur where redistributive policies are aimed at alleviating poverty and promoting equality, or where environmental, cultural and political changes are aimed at increasing the sum of human happiness.

4.2 Growth by trade in primary products

Advantages
- Uses traditional skills.
- Provides basic raw materials.
- Requires low-level skills.

Disadvantages
- Output of renewable resources is variable, e.g. agriculture.
- Output of non-renewable resources can receive a price shock by a new discovery.
- The country may be over-reliant on one product.
- Primary product prices are volatile as supply and demand curves are relatively inelastic.

A solution to this has been the use of buffer stocks to stabilise prices.

Import substitution is more popular politically because it means a country is producing the goods it needs with home industries. However, working long hours with low wages to produce goods for rich consumers in other parts of the world seems to have been better for economic growth.

4.3 Growth by trade in manufactured products

Import substitution: the collapse of world trade in the 1930s led many countries to distrust the stability of export earnings and consider the possibility of import substitution behind quota and tariff barriers.

Countries that chose import substitution seem to have been less successful than those that chose exported growth.

Export-led growth: following the success of Japan, many other countries, particularly in South East Asia, have grown at relatively fast rates through selling consumer durables to the more developed world.

4.4 Development through borrowing

In retrospect, this seems to have been a dangerous way of bringing about economic expansion. Many LDCs have found themselves in **debt crises** as the result of unexpectedly high interest rates, oil price shocks and fluctuating demand for their exports.

4.5 Development through aid

Aid has been criticised for producing a culture of **dependency**. At its worst, aid has been described as 'the poor people in rich countries giving money to the rich people in poor countries'.

Over recent years there has been growing support for the **'trade not aid'** approach. More developed countries are being encouraged to open up their markets to LDCs. There are many difficult barriers, especially those associated with the Common Agricultural Policy.

It has been said that many LDCs would forego all aid for a free opportunity to sell to the **consumers** of the more developed world.

4.6 The Millennium Development Goals

At the Millennium Summit in September 2000, the United Nations agreed the following goals:
- eradicate extreme poverty and hunger
- achieve universal primary education
- promote gender equality
- reduce child mortality
- improve maternal health
- combat HIV/AIDS, malaria and other diseases
- ensure environmental sustainability
- develop a global partnership for development

4.7 Concluding points

In theory, a straightforward solution to inequality would be the free migration of peoples from the poor to the rich countries. This would increase the land and capital per head of the remaining population.

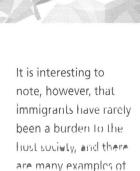
It is interesting to note, however, that immigrants have rarely been a burden to the host society, and there are many examples of them being the most productive group in their new country

In reality, there are two problems. First, the people who leave may be the young and enterprising. Second, the more developed world has established sophisticated welfare and benefit systems which they protect through immigration barriers. The fear is that settlers from the LDCs would flood the system and make it unworkable.

5 Models of economic development

5.1 Rostow's model

This divides the growth model into five stages.
- traditional society
- pre-conditions for take-off
- the take-off
- the drive to maturity
- mass consumption

5.2 The Harrod–Domar model

A one-sector growth model which, in the Keynesian tradition, looks at the role of savings and investment in terms of:
- capital accumulation
- aggregate demand
- aggregate supply
- the accelerator

5.3 The Lewis–Fei–Ranis model

Put forward by A. Lewis in the 1950s, and developed by Fei and Ranis in the 1960s, this model assumes a dual economy with a subsistence agricultural sector and a developing industrial (manufacturing) sector. The industrial sector is the engine of growth that absorbs the surplus agricultural workers.

5.4 Dependency theories

A group of theories which look at the relationship between the more developed world and the less developed world, and how the trade in ideas as well as products promotes economic development. Alternatively referred to as a dependency that leads to the development of peripheral capitalism.

5.5 Balanced and unbalanced growth theories

There is a debate between economists about whether growth is more likely to take place when real variables grow at the same constant rate or if the very nature of imbalance in an economy will bring about a more efficient reallocation of resources.

As the measures move from growth measures to development measures, so they include more items which are difficult to measure in terms of money and require estimates which are difficult to agree upon.

6 Measuring economic growth and development

- **GDP** and **GNP** are probably the most popular measures for economic growth, but there are difficulties in using these statistics for comparison and they have been criticised for not telling the whole story.
- The **Human Development Index** (HDI) was presented in 1990 by the United Nations as an alternative measure for economic development and includes GDP per capita, education (literacy and school enrolment) and life expectancy.
- The **Measure of Economic Welfare** (MEW) was put forward by W. Nordhaus and J. Tobin in 1972. It began with GNP, but made additions for the value of production in the informal economy and leisure time and deductions for environmental damage and travel time to work.
- The **Index of Sustainable Economic Welfare** (ISEW) is used by the Friends of the Earth. Building upon the MEW, the Friends of the Earth try to measure genuine increases in the quality of life with additions for unpaid household labour and deductions for air pollution, great income inequality, a wider interpretation of environmental damage and depletion of resources.

7 Development, sustainability and the carbon footprint

For economic growth and development to be sustainable, the needs and aspirations of the current generation must be met without compromising the anticipated needs of future generations.

It is easy to see how the use of non-renewable resources, environmental damage to the world's flora and fauna, and external costs that seem to be highest in the world's fastest-growing economies threaten sustainability.

In order to increase awareness of the need to protect the environment, there is a measure of the potential for environmental damage which uses the concept of the carbon footprint. Economic activities are measured in terms of carbon dioxide emissions. There is:

- a primary footprint, which measures direct carbon dioxide emissions from energy consumption and transportation
- a secondary footprint, which is an indirect measure of carbon dioxide emissions throughout the whole life cycle of products and waste disposal

The Kyoto Protocol has established targets and timetables for the reduction of greenhouse gas emissions, encouraged carbon offsetting activities such as tree planting, and has promoted of an awareness of the footprint through activities such as the carbon label on products, which was introduced in the UK by the Carbon Trust in 2007.

F Globalisation

1 What is globalisation?

Globalisation is the process that is creating what some commentators have referred to as the 'global village'. This is a world in which products move ever more quickly, people communicate face to face over the internet when they are separated by thousands of miles, ideas flow around the world on a communication network that is not controlled as many countries would like, and money flows across international borders with little restriction.

2 Causes of globalisation

2.1 Reduction in transport costs

It is now possible to move people around the world more cheaply, hence an explosion of tourism that promotes integration among people. You can order something in Hong Kong and have it delivered 24 hours later in London. It is also possible to fragment the production process using cheap labour in one part of the world and skilled labour in another part of the world.

2.2 Reduction in communication costs

The transfer of ideas around the world is quicker and cheaper that it ever was as the result of the internet. Loosely affiliated groups can get together and trade ideas with members spread across the globe. Applications a such as Skype allow free communication across the world.

2.3 Reduction in trade barriers

Developments in technology are bypassing traditional restrictions on trade, while international organisations such as the General Agreement on Tariffs and Trade (GATT), which was superseded by the World Trade Organization (WTO), are concerned with facilitating free trade across the world and breaking down barriers between national and supranational bodies.

2.4 Increase in multinational corporations

Some multinational corporations are bigger than some of the small countries in the world, and these corporations span the globe with their production methods and marketing strategies. They take advantage of economies of scale and scope by utilising labour-intensive production techniques in the less developed world and capital-intensive techniques in the more developed world.

2.5 Deregulation of financial markets

Since the 'Big Bang', which deregulated the City of London in 1986, there have been a series of restriction-removing activities across the world. These have allowed capital to flow more freely and multinationals to develop more rapidly.

3   *The impact of globalisation*

3.1 The benefits

3.1a Promoting growth and development

Economies of scale, increases in efficiency, rises in personal disposable income and growing government revenues have resulted from economic growth and globalisation. This accumulation of wealth and rising incomes has allowed economic development to take place across many countries.

3.1b Alleviating poverty and creating greater equality

The increase in demand for labour in areas of the world where it is relatively cheap has created an expectation of rising incomes as skills and the quality of labour improves. Without doubt, the fastest-growing areas of the world, e.g. India and China, were areas where cheap labour first attracted multinational companies to expand and grow their profit margins. Capitalism has been, and still is, one of the greatest engines for equalising incomes over the longer term.

3.1c Creating more tolerance and less conflict

Intolerance and conflict impose economic costs upon society. Greater commu-nication and more awareness of the rest of the world tends to reduce intolerance and conflict and therefore is a definite economic benefit to the world economy.

3.2 Costs

3.2a Externalities

Different rules and regulations around the world could encourage firms to locate where costs are lowest and environmental concerns are less important than achieving fast rates of economic growth. The increase in pollution in China is an obvious example.

In the 2008 Olympics, it was thought necessary to stop cars driving in Beijing for several days before the opening ceremony, in order to reduce pollution levels for athletes.

3.2b Exclusion and conflict

A little more knowledge about other parts of the world may encourage various groups to think that they are excluded from their share of the world's resources, or may promote thoughts about the decadence of the western world or produce religious conflict, all of which impose real costs on the efficient allocation of scarce resources.

3.2c Crime and loss of political control

A good illustration of this is the way in which the internet crosses national boundaries and facilitates, for example, crime in the form of identity theft. Over recent years, this has cost the world economy millions, if not billions of pounds.